THE POWER OF POETRY

THE FUTURE · HOPE · DREAMS · POWER · IDENTITY · POLLUTION · BULLYING · DISCRIMINATION · DESTRUCTION · DISASTER · WAR · POVERTY · EQUALITY

Future Voices

Edited By Debbie Killingworth

First published in Great Britain in 2023 by:

 Young**Writers**

Young Writers
Remus House
Coltsfoot Drive
Peterborough
PE2 9BF
Telephone: 01733 890066
Website: www.youngwriters.co.uk

Printed and bound in the UK by BookPrintingUK
Website: www.bookprintinguk.com
YB0527F

FOREWORD

Since 1991, here at Young Writers we have celebrated the awesome power of creative writing, especially in young adults where it can serve as a vital method of expressing their emotions and views about the world around them. In every poem we see the effort and thought that each student published in this book has put into their work and by creating this anthology we hope to encourage them further with the ultimate goal of sparking a life-long love of writing.

Our latest competition for secondary school students, **The Power of Poetry,** challenged young writers to consider what was important to them and how to express that using the power of words. We wanted to give them a voice, the chance to express themselves freely and honestly, something which is so important for these young adults to feel confident and listened to. They could give an opinion, highlight an issue, consider a dilemma, impart advice or simply write about something they love. There were no restrictions on style or subject so you will find an anthology brimming with a variety of poetic styles and topics. We hope you find it as absorbing as we have.

We encourage young writers to express themselves and address subjects that matter to them, which sometimes means writing about sensitive or contentious topics. If you have been affected by any issues raised in this book, details on where to find help can be found at
www.youngwriters.co.uk/info/other/contact-lines

CONTENTS

Avenue Centre For Education, Luton

Anderson McMaster (12)	62
Sonnie Fitchett (12)	63
Esa Khan (13)	64
Jerry Gerard (13)	65
Julieann Spring (14)	66
Kian Hannah (15)	67
Katie Mcalpine (15)	68
Alexandra Varga (14)	69
Cheyenne Caines (13)	70
Jakub Kulaga (15)	71
Elton Watts (12)	72
Nicholas Bujor (12)	73
Kayden Hannah (12)	74

Basil Paterson Middle School, Edinburgh

P A Harkes (15)	75
G Newman (15)	76
RC Scott (15)	77
Est Gray (15)	78
E de Prey (15)	79
A Plaskon (15)	80
Z Hunter (15)	81

Blacon High School, Blacon

Max Pinches (13)	82
Taylor Williams (14)	84
Lena Witkowska (13)	85
Harry Giles (13)	86
William Buckley (13)	87
Ella Blythin (13)	88
Harry Bennion (13)	89
Ethan Thompson (11)	90
Henrietta Jones (11)	91
George Thomas Davies (13)	92
Molly Robinson (13)	93
Harry Kidd (13)	94
Bailey Barlow (11)	95
Alex Crimes (13)	96

Jess Jones (11)	97
Layla Coldrick (13)	98

Braeview Academy, Dundee

Nairn Mitchell (14)	99
Dawid Wloch (14)	100
Jamie Minto (14)	102
Ellis Milne (14)	104
Ava Means (14)	106
Mathew Brady (14)	108
Alex Thoms (14)	110
Alicia Curran (14)	111
Ryan Weir (14)	112
Ava Finnon (13)	113
Lily Mitchell (13)	114

Copley Academy, Stalybridge

Eliza Igo (13)	115
Ethan Mcguinness (11)	116
Archie Taylor (11)	118
Brooke Dickson (13)	119
Isaac John Matthews (11)	120
Gracie-Leigh Mann (11)	121
Tia Hadfield (13)	122
Jack Yates (11)	123
Jaimee Platt (12)	124
Rubyann Burrows (11)	125
Jodie Green (12)	126
Eva Milhench (11)	127
Isabelle Fisher-Gould (12)	128
Brooke Tracey (11)	129
Amanta Elizabath (13)	130
Tia Holding (11)	131
Zack Ryan	132
Phoebe Payton (11)	133
Ruby Leckey (11)	134
Maddison Bowden (11)	135
Luke Walker (13)	136
Jack Fernley (11)	137
Arlo Woodman (12)	138
Megan Seager (12)	139
Zachary Hafford (11)	140

Nathan Wilson (13)   141

Harrogate Ladies' College, Harrogate

Valeria Munoz Yeregui (12)   142
Scarlett Wright (12)   143
Rose Smalley (12)   144
Poppy Bo Man (12)   145
Isabel Badger (12)   146
Lyra Javed (12)   147
Rosie Kelly (12)   148
Jasmin Rhodes (13)   149
Florence Coyle (12)   150

Holmer Green Senior School, Holmer Green

Natalia Creese (12)   151
Ivy-Rose Gleeson (11)   152
Freddie Phillips (12)   154
Jacob Goldsmith (11)   157
Lola Harris (12)   158
Owen Turner (11)   160
Jenna Kerr (13)   161
Charlie Vittle (12)   162
Yusuf Shaker (12)   164
Heidi Neville (13)   165
Jamie Kearvell (12)   166
Jessica Lewington (13)   167
Gabriella Ramdeen   168
Imogen Blackwell (12)   169
Freya Owen   170
Reece Herbst (11)   171
Georgia Spinks-Gillen (14)   172
Harry Ratcliffe (12)   173
Lily Dell (12)   174
Ava Spencer (11)   175
Elisabeth Last (12)   176
Charlie Pisani (11)   177
Harry Edwards   178
Tom Mule   179
Ezaan Qureshi   180
Chester Styles   181

Oliver Sendall (12)   182
Maisie Lomas (11)   183
Lexie Vaughan (13)   184
Nyiema Kidby (13)   185
Mia James (12)   186
Felix Richardson (11)   187
Ethan Odiam (12)   188
Isla Worth   189
Alicia Spinks-Gillen (12)   190
Harrison Garrett (11)   191
Katie Bickerton (12)   192
Ericka Fiske (12)   194
George Smith (12)   195
Bobby Ardren (12)   196
Jayna Thohan (12)   197
Sophie Osborne (12)   198
Hugo Scott-White (11)   199
Josh Fallon (12)   200
Lucy Titchmarsh (11)   201
Sophia Arshad (13)   202
Jack Mahoney (11)   203
Iqra Iqbal (12)   204
Jessica Macdonald (11)   205
Annabelle Houghton (11)   206
Ruben Myburgh (12)   207
Skye Hopkins (11)   208
Ayaan Qureshi (11)   209
Niall Messer (12)   210
Zaina Ahmed (13)   211
Anna Lacey (12)   212
Dylan Whitticase (11)   213
Archie Groves (11)   214
Yasmin Arshad (12)   215
Oliver Edwards (11)   216
Alishba Mudassar (11)   217
Megan Howse (12)   218
Jude Stenning (11)   219
Archie Fairchild (12)   220
Aaivee-Elizabeth Kelly (11)   221
William Fiske (13)   222
Grace Porter (13)   223
Izzy Beaumont (11)   224
Joe Latham (12)   225

THE
POEMS

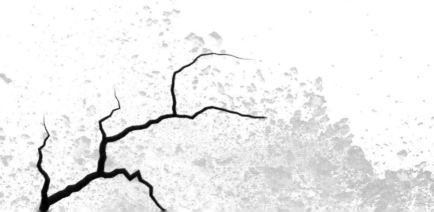

And Still We Do Nothing

The world is warming, the seas are rising
And still we do nothing.
Trees are falling, forests are burning
And still we do nothing.
Death is spreading, bombs are dropping
And still we do nothing.
People are breeding,
Blood is spilling
And still we do nothing.
The sky is falling
But will we do something?

Nicole Nicholson (13)

From Road To Road And Tree To Tree

Please get your plastic out of the sea
Our lawns are all barren, our trees are all dead
Please get this laziness out of your head
Everywhere I look there's smoke
Please save our planet, this isn't a joke
There's plastic and rubbish all over our streets
And big plastic bottles and fast food receipts
There's poison and chemicals in our rivers and seas
They're ooey and gooey just like a disease
From road to road and tree to tree
Please get your plastic out of the sea.

Emilia Grace Mills (11)
ACS International School, Cobham

The Injustice Of Racism

Have you ever thought about what racism actually means?
Imagine what it's like to be the victim
Don't let others feel that way.
Include all, no matter how different.
There is only one race, the human race.
Human rights are everybody's rights.
Stop, listen and act.
Now is the time.
Spread the word because everyone deserves to be treated the same.

Amal Siddiqui (12)
ACS International School, Cobham

How Dare You?

World damage.
Destruction of lives.
Useless waste.
Harmed wildlife.
Nothing...

Dash Hasebe (10)
ACS International School, Cobham

Our Planet

Every day, you hear people say,
One word we all know,
Animals.
But they say it in a way,
As if they are not important
I shall tell you otherwise...

Open your door, go outside,
What do you see?
Humans.
You could see a road and a roadside,
A big city, town, village,
An aeroplane, some rubbish and a field of cows?

What you should see,
Is this -
Nature
A towering tree, the wide sea,
Grasslands and plains,
Birds and beasts alike.

The reason you don't,
Is plain
Crisis
Cutting down lots of trees,
Heating, polluting, littering the Earth,
Killing the animals that only this planet has.

We need to stop.
Help our planet
Enjoy it,
Love it,
Save it,
Appreciate it,
Be proud of it,
It's ours.
We need it,
Nobody can help it on their own
We need to work together

Who is in with me so that we are
Safe?

Gabriella Inglis-Downes (11)
Adcote School For Girls, Little Ness

Extinction

Wolves, the ancestors of dogs
Our beloved friends
Who never fail to defend
When they think we are in trouble

The Ethiopian wolf, guilty for nothing more
Than killing its prey when searching for
The food it needs, to keep its pack alive
Yet human habitat destruction
Rabies, poachers and farm construction
Has killed off the many wolves
Who would have survived

The red wolf, one of the smallest wolves in the family
of canines,
Reduced to less than thirty by the hunts
The brutal and barbaric injustice of the poaching of noble
creatures
Our nation experiencing bliss

By comparison.
Unknowing and uncaring that innocent animals
Are being shot for no adequate reason
The worst of some people's worries is what's in fashion
this season.

By 1926, wolves were gone from Yellowstone
For every wolf, North America became a danger zone
The Lamar Canyons, the Druid Peaks,
Each and every wolf unique

The grey wolf was banished
The elk numbers grew
They overgrazed the land,
Eating trees and shrubs too
The willows and aspens stopped growing and died
The songbird population began to decline
The wolves were crucial to the ecosystem
And Doug Smith campaigned to bring them back
What also helped convince people, was the 1973
Endangered Species Act.
After years of heated discussions
They began the reintroduction
To wolves in Yellowstone.

They are vital to our environment
Yet people are still leading hunts
Against the innocent animal.
What does it take to make people see
That wolves have a role that has always been
Crucial to nature as we know it
Nature, which is slowly being harmed,
Right at this minute
As deforestation and pollution

Make our planet more unhealthy,
We are heading towards a future
With an unbearably hot humidity.
How do you feel in the middle of a heatwave?
Multiply that by hundreds,
And decide whether that's the path you want to take.

Magali Towers (11)
Adcote School For Girls, Little Ness

A World Inside My Head

A row of endless corridors
Made of never-ending doors
Every time I head inside
I'm greeted with lies upon lies
Every time
Every day
I eat lime and stay
At home, awaiting my dismay
The sour memories
Turn into stories
Of old libraries
All about wars
Which are all supplied
In these stuffed halls
Of pain behind
Every door
Every floor
Causes me uproar
I feel like I can't take it anymore
Although there were many warriors
All of which tried
The pain that they had worn
Caused them to have flied
As I walked past
Every library

Trapped in my head
With nothing but misery
That was all until
An exit was seen
A door was there built
To leave I was keen
All I needed was a key
A key to destiny
And I had known

Exactly where it's placed
Ready to embrace

The row of endless corridors
Made of never-ending doors
Except this time I went inside
Greeted with times upon times
Every memory
Every story
Held a part of destiny
And spread out were little acts
That seemed to make me happy
Every memory
Every story
Held a part of the key
The key
To my destiny

Hajer Al-Dalla Ali (13)
Al-Islah Girls' High School, Blackburn

Run Away With Me

Everyone seems happy but me
Laughing hurts more than crying
Sometimes I wish to escape this world

When I saw you, the magic had started
Run away with me, run away with me
Across the sky to the end of the world
When we're together, time stops-
Everything instilled around us
Let's make a spell with our tears
So we can stay like this forever
At the edge is my burning heart
But I just want to stay

Run away with me to a magic island
A magic island where glittering visions turn into reality
Let's leave this ashen city behind
And keep it our little secret
Can you be my eternity?

Wishing upon the star
The catalyst to our adventures
Blusterous winds grazing against us
Nothing holding us back
Glistening starlit nights engulf us
Our hearts running wild

Let's follow the melody
Sparkled with dreams to the very end
Nothing hurts more than going back
To that tainted world
So why don't you run away with me?

Shahina Hajat
Al-Islah Girls' High School, Blackburn

This Is Spring

As spring blooms into the year
The memories of last winter are forgotten
The birds chirp and sing
Watching the sunset prelude into dawn
It was indeed springtime
A season filled with new life
The season where leaves would sway agilely
Following the cool breeze once more
Hypnotising yet intoxicating, this is spring

However, last winter's snow has remained
Entirely submerging my heart
Oh, what should I do?
When my enclosed heart is unable to bounce free
Filled with exhilaration at the arrival of spring
The memories we once shared had flown away
With the howling wind
Unable to be caught, slipping through my fingers
As if they were meant to be forgotten

The real purpose of spring
Is to bestow hope among the young and old
By showing the flames light the sky
That had once been extinguished from their hearts
It's almost like love at first sight
It enters and starts gracefully

But sooner than later, bids its farewell
In the end, it's just numbness which remains.

Sana Alam (14)
Al-Islah Girls' High School, Blackburn

Interchange

Many times, we have witnessed the hatred, the injustice
between people.
This life we once had was a dream we thought would
last forever.
But then a change in humanity, equality and punctuality...
Faces change every day.
This Earth never stops turning... or does it stop for anyone?
Change this life back to the days we laughed, smiled
and cried.
The days we thought were on pause.
But then suddenly, someone pressed 'skip'...
A big bang shook the Earth to a bigger change like a
lightning bolt that struck the Earth.
People's faces changed; life changed.
I may not be a mathematician or technician,
But I can tell you there will come a day where the universe,
life and its people will have its back on you.
So be the mountain that your problems seem to cling to.
Take hold of the people that bring you down.
Show them what the truth is, show them the life we once
had. Because this Earth never stops turning or does it stop
for anyone?

Sarmina Najeeb (13)
Al-Islah Girls' High School, Blackburn

The Dark Side Of The World

Have you ever wondered what is the reason why over one
million animals die a year?
Well one reason is caused by us,
We can't keep mess to ourselves and make a fuss,
Something called littering.
The effects of this is triggering.
This must stop.

Do you know what causes thousands of deaths?
Air pollution.
To this chaos, there must be a solution.
This problem is caused by everyday things,
Plenty of damage, air pollution brings.
This must stop.

Why is bullying so common?
One example is identity and many more.
People won't care and ignore,
Bullying exists in almost every school.
People could be bullied because they aren't 'cool'.
This must stop!

Khulaybah Mahroosh (12)
Al-Islah Girls' High School, Blackburn

Climate Change

The government are not with us but let's make a change.
Let's stand together, work together and let's make a big change in this world.
Plastic straws, plastic bottles are bad for this environment.
Stop littering, stop making people's lives harder.
There are many animals that are dying because of this environment.
We need to make sure every animal on this planet is living.
Everything is changing,
Make a change quick!
Recycle, recycle, recycle!
We need to stop littering.
Grab your litter pickers.
Pick up as much as you can.
Don't forget about paper and glass.
Recycle together, with your entire class.
So take time out on Earth Day to show the world you care!

Safa Ali (12)
Al-Islah Girls' High School, Blackburn

Bullying 101

B ullying is not funny, it's not a joke.

U ttering mean comments to others about your folk.

L aughing at people because of what they wear.

L aughing at others, this isn't fair.

Y ou can't just be mean to others, they have feelings too.

I know bullying is always overlooked, but please we need you.

N o one should ever experience this.

G o tell someone if you are getting bullied.

Bullying even leads to suicide.

This is really important.

Is this what you really want?

Our population is decreasing just by this.

Is that what you wish?

Why can't we just be nicer?

Aalia Dhorat (12)
Al-Islah Girls' High School, Blackburn

Nature

Nature is calming and a peaceful word
It comprises of trees animals and birds
We have learnt to call a mother nature
But sadly, all we do is ruthless torture

Look up at the trees...
Hearing and singing of the birds
Happily chirping without words

The gift of God, the Almighty Lord
The sky, the clouds
And the winter with fog
The morning and the night
A beautiful moonlight then the bright sunlight
The sunrise the sunset

The horizon on the Earth is stretched
The beauty of nature is no one can ever match
The deserts, the hill station
The gardens and the orchards
The fruit and the flowers
That the plants and the trees bear
This is the beauty of nature...
Extinguishing and rare.

Hafsa Noor
Al-Islah Girls' High School, Blackburn

The Book Room

Far away, yet close by
Is a place where many books lie
Rows and rows, aisles and aisles
The words are tucked away and filed

Chaos echoes through the space
Deafening, silent - then absent
Flick through the pages, there is a trace
Of stories - past, future and present

I pull off a book from one of the shelves
I see memories, moments and thoughts
The text I read tells
Of things of many sorts

Bright, innocent, happy
Dark, guilty, sad
Feelings, not memories
Reminisce moments, good and bad

Day by day, life goes on
The chapter commences; life's trials
Are illustrated. The book is restored
Back to the original, organised aisles.

Tahirah Begum (15)
Al-Islah Girls' High School, Blackburn

2022

8th September 2022 was a very tragic day
This is when the Queen unfortunately passed away
She reigned for 70 years
Sadly we lost her this year
She was a lovely and caring Queen
She wore green in this year's Jubilee
Elizabeth ruled 14 countries
And she loved her lovelies
She helped people a lot
Which we appreciate more than a lot
Some people were sad
Some people were mad
When we heard the news
Which was kind of new
Our hearts broke
And it upset all sorts of folk
Her last shake was with Liz Truss
Queen Elizabeth always trusted us
Rest in peace, Queen Lizzy.

Irfah Ahmed (12)
Al-Islah Girls' High School, Blackburn

Winter Evening

On a cloudy evening, right after it snowed
I'm out in the forest just to catch the scene

I watch the trees, I watch the leaves
As they flow with the cold breeze on this winter evening

I can take the cold, I can take the snow
I'm out in the forest just roaming and flowing

White, lifeless, cold like a cloud
I'm out here chilling on this winter evening

I think of the snow when I'm up in Marquette
The only time you see me smiling is when the white
snow is setting

What more can you ask for? The white snow?
You complain about the cold
While here I am living.

Jannat Khalid (14)
Al-Islah Girls' High School, Blackburn

1952

Unfortunately, Elizabeth's father passed away
It happened whilst she was on holiday
Sadly it was too late to say her goodbyes
She was left to sigh and cry
When she became Queen
She ruled over 14 countries
Jamaica, Canada, New Zealand and Africa
These are only some of the countries
She was also so funny
She met many people throughout her reign
Including the president of Ukraine
She also met Paddington Bear
Which is very rare.
She was a lovely Queen
She was never mean
This is why we all loved the Queen.

Aisha Aden (12)
Al-Islah Girls' High School, Blackburn

Change

The world is changing
What should we do?
From littering to plastic
Let's make the world fantastic
And show what we can do.

The streets are a mess
So, let's make this less
To make it clean
Is a never-before scene
And show what we can do.

We should be grateful
For what we have
To see people on the streets
Feeling cold and wanting some heat
So, let's make the world compete
And show what we can do.

No one should feel bad about their skin
Or feel like they belong in a garbage bin
No fighting, an all-free zone
No kid fighting alone
So, let's show what we can do.

Khadija Hussain (12)
Al-Islah Girls' High School, Blackburn

Do You Ever Wonder...?

Do you ever wonder how many children get bullied?
Do you ever wonder how many children commit suicide?
Do you ever wonder how many children fake a smile
on their faces?
Do you ever wonder how many children compare
themselves?
Do you ever wonder how many children starve themselves?
This is all because of social media and bullying.
We need to make a change.
We need to stop bullying
We need to stop making people feel insecure.
We need to stop comparing.
We need to stop suicide.
We need to make a change!

Laibah Waseem (12)
Al-Islah Girls' High School, Blackburn

2021

Prince Philip who died in 2021
Was the Queen's number one,
When he died
He was 99,
The Queen named him as her rock,
He loved the Queen a lot.
When the Prince died,
The Queen could not leave his side.
She cried and cried,
And was left with a sigh.
Prince Philip had a good life,
And he left us with a lot of rights.
The prince was loved by a lot of people
But we never know if he did anything illegal.
The Prince had an amazing life,
This is a poem of the Prince's fact file.

Hafsah Mulla (12)
Al-Islah Girls' High School, Blackburn

The Planet Isn't A Joke

The planet isn't a joke,
We can't keep playing,
It's time to make a change,
Thousands of chemicals are released into the air,
Children coughing all around the world.
The planet isn't a joke,
It's time to make a change.
Thousands of animals going extinct,
If we change our environment we could make a change.

By putting our waste in the right bin
It creates a better environment for our animals.
Stop throwing plastic on the streets
Because our planet isn't a joke.

Dua Nawaz (12)
Al-Islah Girls' High School, Blackburn

Suffering But Smiling

In the boundless abyss of my languished spirit
My throttled soul, ever so fragile
A decayed heart, tinged with bittersweet
The silent weeping cloaked with a smile
Discarded in the debris of the Earth itself
The carcass of mine drenched in blood
The notion itself disoriented in a chasm
This artificial universe, ever so misleading
Abandoned I am - cut off the edge
Though nothing remains, my incessant figure is still present
My agitation has led me to hysterical dismay
An immoral tragedy that cursed my conscience
Will neglect me till my last day.

Haadiyah Rizwan (14)
Al-Islah Girls' High School, Blackburn

Life Without Light

Deep within my withered soul
All I see is an empty hole
People going against you and breaking your heart
Then your evil traits begin to start
People wonder where your smile has gone
Just let them know that darkness has finally won
I want to live to tell them that I've been a soldier in this war
And that it was never easy to overcome
Your painted heart goes ice-cold
And then someone else's story will be told
You slowly begin to drown and drift away
And you realise when it's too late.

Hifza Akhtar (13)
Al-Islah Girls' High School, Blackburn

Climate Change

It is difficult for us to escape
We're running out of time to get out safely.

Our planet is undergoing a climatic change
So let's recycle plastic, glass and others
Because climate change is not peaceful but terrifying.

I know climate change may be frightening
But to save this planet we need to recycle.

Our Earth is melting,
Our Earth is crumbling,
Our Earth is grumbling.

Everyone is capable of making change
So let's do it!

Momna Arif (14)

Al-Islah Girls' High School, Blackburn

Starlight

Hold my hand, let me dream about you
Look at the alluring constellation and such an
illuminating exhibit
Starlight shining brighter than the darkest night
The later the night gets, the brighter the starlight

The heavens above, an incredible scenery
There's a whole new world waiting for us
I wonder what it would feel like migrating to this world

Let's capture every beautiful and memorable moment
of our life
Just don't let go of my hand
Don't wake up from this dream.

Zainab Tauseef (13)
Al-Islah Girls' High School, Blackburn

Coronavirus

We can't touch
But I can't reach out.
We hunker down
But we still rise up.
Our bodies are attacked
But our spirits fight back.
The enemy is invisible
But so many of our heroes are now seen.

Weeks and weeks of isolation
But still infinite and invincible determination.
We are distant
But we stand together.
And together
We shall overcome.
I believe I can
And I know you can.

Malikah Jan (12)
Al-Islah Girls' High School, Blackburn

The Cost-Of-Living Crisis

Inflation the highest in 40 years,
Which gave many people tears
And a lot of fears,
Which made many give up their beers,
That didn't lead to cheers.

An increase on shopping, bills and fuel,
What they have done is so cruel,
I don't think they should rule,
This isn't so cool.

Lifestyle is changing,
People are raging,
Which isn't quite amazing
And not at all praising.

This needs to stop,
Prices need to drop,
So, people can shop
Non-stop!

Aisha Hussain (12)
Al-Islah Girls' High School, Blackburn

Reach Your Goal

You're in control of your destiny
Alongside none
Build your path creatively
And check off things that must be done

There's no limit to what you can achieve
There are no barriers to stop you from pursuing your dream
Never let go of your desires, always believe
For everything is not as it seems

The moment you take responsibility for your life
The more you work on your passions
You begin to see yourself thrive
Avoid distractions
And reach your goal.

Alishba Shah (15)
Al-Islah Girls' High School, Blackburn

Changing The World

Let's make a change to our universe.
It's time to play our part
And stop this bad environment.
Let's stop this bad habit,
Throwing our plastic in the wrong bins.
Let's make a change altogether.
We could do this if we tried and tried to look after our
environment.
Let's stop this war once and for all.
Let's make a change.

Hafsa Abdullah (12)
Al-Islah Girls' High School, Blackburn

Raindrops

R aindrops fall from grey, dull clouds
A gain and again, they fall to the ground
I n the streets, on the roads
N o one to play with, no one to get cold
D rizzling, drizzling
R ain, rain, rain
O pen your arms, feel nature
P ray the sun will come later
S o surely after, you will feel greater.

Anisa Mahmood (13)

Al-Islah Girls' High School, Blackburn

The World Today

The smoky skies, the horrible air,
People on the planet don't seem to care.
In the world today
Beautiful days are never seen,
The world today is never clean.

The nations seem not to care about the world,
They need to raise awareness about this situation
Because this can ruin our nations.

Maryam Nisar (12)
Al-Islah Girls' High School, Blackburn

The Longest-Reigning Queen

She was the longest-reigning Queen,
She was always seen,
She was very funny,
She had lots of money.

She was Queen in 1952,
She was always true,
She was very bold,
This was always told.

Safiyyah Mulla (12)
Al-Islah Girls' High School, Blackburn

Sticks And Stones

Who inspires you? they ask
and I can give a lot answers,
there are people who make music
people who give answers,
they help me understand myself more than I know,
and they don't care about race because does that
even matter?
Our current time is going mad with racism and anger,
no one understands we need to take action,
because people who want to inspire can also tend to give
wrong points, the points of anger,
but when one little thing goes wrong, the whole world is
on their back
people can't seem to think about the way that
people change,
they take something from ten years ago and make
it big today,
so why should you listen to others when you could
be yourself?
You need to stop focusing on others and focus on yourself,
because no one thinks anymore
all they do is type because they seem to think hurting
people's emotions is alright,
they don't understand everyone fights their own fights,
and the fact they just let what happens happen because of
the people being bullied...

"Yeah, they're alright!"
But did you know that Tim down the road hurt himself
last night
because the bullying and hate and the pressure made him
want to change his appetite?
Now he hardly eats no more just because of it
maybe just maybe think about your actions,
get it in your head that you can take your own action,
why can't you understand that sticks and stones, yeah they
break bones
but the words, they can also last forever!

James Skinner (15)
Aurora Hedgeway School, Pilning

Earth

On a planet named Earth, dark green trees wait in the frosty wind,
Whilst the dozy donkeys and the sleepy monkeys sleep in the overgrown gaps of the forest.

The frozen lake which lies on the opposite side of the Earth cracks
Whilst the fish jump and steal the seagull's chips.

Opposite the lake, there is a cave, where all sorts of snorts echo.
In some fields on the other side of the cave,
there are red, green and orange juicy fruits growing
off the hedges.

Which are on the edge of a horizon.
The sun shines and the sea glitters in the reflection of a boy's mirror
which is placed in his bedroom window.

His cosy bed makes me want to sleep.
The view from his balcony is nothing but beauty and colours.

In the sky, the similar planets shine but that's for another day.

Marley Bull (12)
Aurora Hedgeway School, Pilning

My Family

My family make me feel safe,
My family is kind and helpful,
My family care for people,
My family make me feel loved,
My family love cuddles,
My family love watching movies,
My family loves chocolates and sweets,
My family like cooking cakes,
My family loves spending time with each other and with
their best friends,
My family is noisy and loud,
My family loves playing badminton,
My family like going on walks,
My family love food,
My family loves making memories together every day.

Gracey Lyons (12)
Aurora Hedgeway School, Pilning

Nature's Love

Nature's love is just like a dove,
You see the trees in the wind,
All light and colourful,
How wonderful the water,
So bright it gives me a fright,
The reflection so pretty,
The snow so white,
And cold and so bold,
The flowers so nice,
I just want to sleep,
With the smell so passionate,
Like satin,
Oh how wonderful nature really is for kids,
The mums have a break
For goodness sake,
The children play in the trees,
On their knees,
Every day is an adventure when you're with me,
We will travel in the sea,
Oh how fun it would be,
So stress-free,
"All your thoughts,
Float away in the wind,
And are never seen again!" said the man,

That's why I love nature,
I hope you do too.

Boe Morton (12)
Aurora Hedgeway School, Pilning

My Interest

Football is all I think about,
I miss it in the summer drought,

Going to the match on game day,
I wish I was on the pitch to play,

Bang the ball into the net,
I worry about people that have placed a bet,

We go to the beautiful game,
To sing and have a good time,

This is why we all love the beautiful game all around,
Gameday clashes with the crowd's cheer sound,

The beautiful ball goes across the pitch,
That is why we love the beautiful game.

Austin Allen (13)
Aurora Hedgeway School, Pilning

War

M achine guns booming through eardrums,
O verkill of the soldiers,
D estruction of the fallen buildings,
E xploding mines under the soil,
R eloading weapons with bullets,
N ear the enemy.

W aiting to strike,
A ttacking the planet,
R unning from the war,
F ighting for their country,
A ssault rifle bullets echoing through the battlefield,
R esist against the enemy,
E nd the war.

Jack Smart (13)

Aurora Hedgeway School, Pilning

Mr Microwave

M r Microwave,

I s very cool,

C an create wishes and he can

R un, cook animals, etc!

O ven bullies Microwave because Microwave is a smaller version of Oven,

W hen they fight their beeping is their censor bar,

"A hahahhhh!" Dave rages while they keep beeping!

V ery good times, he can't hear their voices, very rarely they get along!

E ven now they fight every day...

Levi Corden (11)
Aurora Hedgeway School, Pilning

The Amazon

N o more homes for animals
A ll will be lost soon
T hey deserve saving
U nited we should be
R espect our planet
A ll should be loved
L et's come together

H appy animals
A re
B eautiful
I want to see the change
T igers eating
A xolotls smiling
T apir grazing
S nakes slithering.

Kyle Thomas (14)
Aurora Hedgeway School, Pilning

Memes That Rhyme (And Are Cool)

Roses are red,
Violets are blue,
A Thomas bomb,
Is speeding towards you

Who does Sonic hate?
Everyone who discriminates!

Oh boy! It's 3am!
Mario time
Don't destroy Big Ben!

I am a crazy prisoner,
I have escaped at last, yes!
If captured again, I'll escape from prison tomorrow too,
To make America a big mess!
Haha!

Jasper Sadler (11)
Aurora Hedgeway School, Pilning

Stop Eating Beans

Jonny was a child who loved eating beans,
Jonny loved them so much he ate them tin by tin by all
means,
Jonny had beans for breakfast,
Jonny had beans for dinner,
Jonny had beans for tea,
Jonny had beans for supper,
Jonny loved them so much he bought himself bean trees,
Jonny's dad was super disappointed,
He hated beans and loved his peas.

Harry Scott (13)
Aurora Hedgeway School, Pilning

The Shadows

You might live in the shadows
I was born in them shadows

Can be anywhere behind you
In front of you, everywhere around you

Sometimes some things might lurk in them shadows

Could be just like a clone of you
A clone of a ship, a clone of an animal

A clone of your mum and dad or friends
Any one of your family members.

Regan Frowen-Young (13)
Aurora Hedgeway School, Pilning

Extinction

This poem starts way before Christ,
Where there were no satellites,
Where dinosaurs weren't stuck in ice,
Where woolly mammoths roamed the ice,
Where sabre-toothed tigers did hunt,
Where T-rexes did jump,
Where giant ground sloths had no fun.

Now come back to the present day,
Where all we can say is cool.

Georgia Box (13)
Aurora Hedgeway School, Pilning

Hail To The Church Of Me

Her eyes light up the skies like my mind never could.
Gentle smiles surround her, how the rocks hug the sea.
Her love so strong it makes me cry.
To see her fly so high to leave my grip.
My mind starts to slip uneasy, uncertain.
Her touch leaves scars as she smiles so cruel.
Goodbye, one last gentle cry lights up the sky.

Callum Barlow (17)
Aurora Hedgeway School, Pilning

Nine Worlds

A dragon was soaring in the sky like a plane,
It was soaring so fast, one of its scales was falling off,
It felt like an eruption from a volcano,
But it crashed and felt like an earthquake,
Another dragon was flying over at the speed of light,
And chucked the crashed dragon right into space.

Castiel Harris (12)
Aurora Hedgeway School, Pilning

Space

J upiter is the 5th planet from the sun,
U nveiled by Babylonian astronomers,
P laced in time 800-700 BC
I like the colours on Jupiter
T emprature is -87°C to - 5°C,
E arth is the 3rd planet from the sun,
R oman king of the gods.

Lacey Godwin (12)
Aurora Hedgeway School, Pilning

The Car

Oh Bryan and Ryan,
two Irish twins from Donegal,
went to buy a VW Golf.
When they arrived at the farm in Wexford,
the bright red car waited,
when Bryan fired it up,
he and Ryan roared back,
home to Donegal,
where it lived until,
it blew up two years later.

Oliver Fry (11)
Aurora Hedgeway School, Pilning

School Bore

School, it is boring, it is cruel,
I'd rather be playing in a pool,
It is snoring, it is boring,
I would rather go to the zoo and see lions roaring,
It is inescapable,
It is capable,
Of sending one to sleep,
And it can make you be silent, not even a peep.

Leo Dunk (11)
Aurora Hedgeway School, Pilning

The Scattering Feet Of Chonkers

The scattering feet of chonkers are heard throughout the halls,
They look so beautiful at all the grand balls,
They are more royal than royalty,
More precious than the Queen's diamonds in her crown,
Their evil plan will begin now,
Can you see it in their frowns?

Arthur Highet (12)
Aurora Hedgeway School, Pilning

Cats

Cats can catch mice,
Cats can climb trees,
Cats can hide,
Cats can miaow,
Cats can hear the smallest sounds,
Cats can purr when they are happy,
Cats can jump,
Cats can run,
Cats can claw paper.

Sam Castle (11)
Aurora Hedgeway School, Pilning

Ninjago

N injago
I like them
N injas are good
J umping ninja
A ninja spin
G oing to go
O h I love Ninjago.

Poppy Carter (12)
Aurora Hedgeway School, Pilning

Gang Violence

G angs
A re unnecessary
N o need for them
G et away from gang life

V arious people are in gangs
I believe people shouldn't be afraid to leave their home
O n top of that gangs also put you in danger
L ots of young people are being groomed into gangs
E veryone can be a victim to gang violence
N obody should feel unsafe
C hoose your life wisely
E veryone has a right to a safe life.

Anderson McMaster (12)

Avenue Centre For Education, Luton

Knife Life

I witnessed a kill
Didn't give me a thrill
Made me feel sick
Made me feel ill.

The guy got hurt
And now he is lying in the dirt
Wasn't his fault
Shouldn't have got murked.

When you use a knife
You can take a life
Could lose a husband
Could lose a life.

I'm writing this song
'Cause knives are wrong
People stay safe
People stay strong.

Sonnie Fitchett (12)
Avenue Centre For Education, Luton

Kill Knives

K nives
N o need to kill using knives
I don't want to see everyone losing lives
F riends and family losing their lives
E veryone needs to be calm and kind

C hildren could get caught with a knife
R uining their whole life
I want to see the world be a safe place
M urder is never the answer
E veryone needs to be calm and kind.

Esa Khan (13)
Avenue Centre For Education, Luton

Get Back Gangs

Gangs are not cool
Go to school you fool
Stop being cruel
For a postcode you don't even rule
Instead, stand in the spotlight
And before you know it, you'll be taking flights
Put away your knife, people should be safe at night
Just go home and make a rhyme
Representing a gang can take away your time
Some people are doing life for committing the crime
Use your time to make a dime.

Jerry Gerard (13)
Avenue Centre For Education, Luton

Cultural Differences

Why do we have to live by certain rules?
Why are girls treated differently to boys?
Why am I not allowed to be who I want to be?

There should be equal rules between girls and boys.
Why are girls treated like toys?
It's not fair how boys get what they demand
Whilst girls have to follow every command.
I want to be an independent individual
Why does the world have to be so cruel?

Julieann Spring (14)
Avenue Centre For Education, Luton

Knives

K illing is not the answer to anything
N ever carry knives
I ntense pressure
F ighting is not right
E veryone deserves to live

C riminals always rot in cells
R ethink before doing it
I njuring people is never the right decision
M others left grieving
E motions run high.

Kian Hannah (15)
Avenue Centre For Education, Luton

Knife Crime

K illing is not the answer
N ever hold weapons
I njuring others is not good
F ind the right thing to do
E veryone's life matters

C rime does not pay
R ethink what you're doing
I ntense pressure by peers
M urder is not the answer
E veryone has the right to live.

Katie Mcalpine (15)

Avenue Centre For Education, Luton

Hairbrush

My mirror's reflection, facing me as I brush my hair,
I know today I'm going to be going somewhere,
Slow as I see the sun rise...
I hesitate and look at the mirror twice,
A bright white light,
I see my figure self standing tall and walking.
I look like a grown-up version of myself.
I am beautiful, just the way I am.

Alexandra Varga (14)
Avenue Centre For Education, Luton

Refuse Racism

R acism is everywhere
A ll colours and races should be treated the same
C olour of your skin shouldn't matter
I n the world we live in people shouldn't be afraid
S o many races and religions are being killed innocently
M any people are scared to say what they believe.

Cheyenne Caines (13)
Avenue Centre For Education, Luton

Money, Money, Money

Money, money, money
Is the owner of the power.
Money, money, money
Are wealthy people sweet or sour?
Money, money, money
Some people make many pounds within an hour.
Money, money, money
Some people work with money, making glass towers.
Money, money, money
Does money really give you power?

Jakub Kulaga (15)
Avenue Centre For Education, Luton

Be Kind

Drugs and knives take civilian lives
All these crimes make the world not nice
Innocent people are trying spice
Drugs and knives are creating gang war fights
Everyone should be safe day and throughout the night when
people are high
Racist thoughts come to mind
People need to learn how to be kind.

Elton Watts (12)
Avenue Centre For Education, Luton

Drugs

D o not use drugs
R uining your life is not the answer
U ndercover police are always prowling
G et help if you feel like you're drowning
S ay no to drugs!

Nicholas Bujor (12)
Avenue Centre For Education, Luton

Violence Is Never The Answer

G angs

A re irrelevant and unnecessary

N egative influences are in gangs

G angs

S top them. Violence is never the answer!

Kayden Hannah (12)
Avenue Centre For Education, Luton

Bunny

I lolloped down the forest path,
My mother by my side.
We smelled the roses that'd grown
Within the endless garden we called our own.
The world she shared with me was filled with beauty
But that didn't stop her from being scared.
I wasn't neighbours with the woodland creatures,
I didn't have any forest friends.
But her biggest concern was always men.
I never understood her fear.
I thought that in a world so divine, trouble could never
be near.
Until one sunny afternoon,
We came across a flowery clearing and played for hours.
My mother told me it was time to leave, but of course, I
wouldn't listen.
I was far too busy, making a fool of myself near the stream,
the one that would glisten.
She shrieked, "Now!" and urged me,
But I thought it was just a game.
I heard a loud gunshot,
Now it's me to blame.
I have no forest friends, despite how much I wished I did.
My last option was to run to my mother,
So the man would get me too.

P A Harkes (15)
Basil Paterson Middle School, Edinburgh

Don't Ski Alone

The mountains are my challenge.
The skis are my pride.
Amongst the trees, I keep my balance -
This one will be a smooth ride.
I swing past a boulder,
But then, I crash into a pine.
I tumble, I bruise my shoulder.
I crumble, I twist my spine.
I lay in the snow, dazzled, in pain.
The sky above is black, a swirling void of forever.
I struggle to stand, there's mist in my brain.
I have to keep going, the mountains I must endeavour.
The coldness is brittle, the snow gathers on my nose.
The creatures of the night call my name and howl.
I stay still but I still hear footsteps, and the fear in me arose.
They get closer, quicker, yet more silent.
A vibration in the air, a low, cruel growl.
Buried in white snow, now red. It tore off my head.
I've been dragged onto a stone. It eats my femur bone.
All my blood I've bled. I lay here forever, dead.
The mountains are cold and cruel. Don't ski alone.

G Newman (15)
Basil Paterson Middle School, Edinburgh

Mother Nature's Creations

When I look out into Zootopia that Mother Nature created
When I look out into the endless green

My mind loses all sense of worry
My mind clear, almost a sense of numbness

The glass clear, rain began to pour on my jacket
Water droplets lay on the grass like a wet coat of paint

Then the leaves flutter off the trees
Like birds taking their first flight

Then the sun peeks behind a cloud
As the warmth and light flood the scene
The small creatures begin to emerge from their habitats

Then I remember that this amazing creation of nature
Is slowly fading away, slowly withering out.
This is the act of the biggest monsters of all
The most dangerous species alive -
Humans.

RC Scott (15)
Basil Paterson Middle School, Edinburgh

Highland Cow

My habitat's undestroyed, beautiful, and bright
It becomes what it needs to be

My habitat's got water smiling at me
The snow falling happily

The green grass, the lambs jumping
Buttercups shining upon us all

The sun shining down
But my habitat changes
It changes for us all

The cold ploughing down upon us
The trees covered in ice
Moss frozen underneath it all

The squirrels jumping branch to branch
Because my habitat changes

My horns as strong as the tide
The stag exploring the land

Clouds above us all changing
Standing tall through it all

Humpback whales peacefully swimming
Eagles majestically soaring
Because our habitat changes.

Est Gray (15)
Basil Paterson Middle School, Edinburgh

Mountain Sickness

A deceiving landscape, the Scottish hills
Bumps along unconcernedly.
Valleys long ago carved into them by a long-forgotten
sculptor.

The heather caught in the swell of the stony waves.
The heather that filled the gap left by an old host.
An ancient forest remaining in the ground and the
memory of stones.
The barren hills pretending to look like they have before.

A landscape dotted with rocks and boulders
And in one glen, a virus spreading, proud of itself infecting,
Admiring the achievement and magnitude of its contagion.
And for the first time the hills themselves feel threatened.

E de Prey (15)
Basil Paterson Middle School, Edinburgh

The Sun, The Moon

The sun, the moon
The sea, the sky

We look up to see a painting of white and blue
And in the night, lights on hues

We turn left to an ocean surrounding our every move
We turn right to a forest filled with dreams and hope

We stand and listen to the birds outside
Till beautiful tunes start to come out

The place we smile, the place we cry
The place we live, the place we love

The sun the moon
The sea, the sky

My heart flutters at this wonderful world
At this world of wonderful things.

A Plaskon (15)
Basil Paterson Middle School, Edinburgh

Rose Garden

Lying in the rose garden
Dewdrops between my fingers
Petals in my hair
Watching the soft clouds float by

Wondering when it will no longer be
So beautiful.

Through the white tattered fence
Flowers emerge, overgrown
Begging to be set free.

As the sun glimmers in the heat
A cool breeze flutters past
Like a butterfly in spring.

This peaceful moment -
It won't last forever.
Nothing does.

The beauty swept away in a puff of smoke.

Z Hunter (15)
Basil Paterson Middle School, Edinburgh

The World Is At War

Men and women cheer as children laugh but then are so
filled with tears as nothing can save them from the monster
that is near.
For the world is at war and children cling on for dear life.
They cling to their mothers.
Their fathers.
But they can't hold on
Because no one can hold on for long.
No one. No one at all.
So they will so be ripped from their clan because the
monster never fails.
For the monster is unforgiving, he is who steals the
children's fathers and brothers but leaves the mothers
to grieve.
To grieve all alone.

And on the next days death will be near.
So he will cheer as his monster roars and its green smoke
will rise.
The sign of death as the monster comes screaming and
shouting ensures that no one will survive.
No one at all.
And on that night
The night where no one survives,
The women will cry as they find out the news.
The news of the killed in action
With this news there is no man coming home

But there is a child now, the new man coming home on
his own.
But not all is lost,
The monster of war has lost
And mankind has prevailed.

Max Pinches (13)
Blacon High School, Blacon

Goodison Park

Here I am once again,
Walking into the lion's den,
Will we cry or will we roar
When the mighty Blues do score?

A sea of blue down Spellow Lane,
Or Toffees going to the game,
Into the fanzone, past Dixie Dean's,
To watch the glory of our team.

Out the rain and into cover,
Through the turnstiles we discover,
A smell of pies, coffees and beer,
As Z Cars play, the crowd will cheer.

Legends have graced the pitch over the years,
Bringing other players to tears,
The Holy Trinity were the best of all,
Harvey, Kendall and Alan Ball.

Taylor Williams (14)
Blacon High School, Blacon

Human Rights

To preserve
Equality and human rights
As humans we must insist
To continue our fights.
As for ourselves these at least
We should reserve.
Is there anything else as human beings
That we so naturally deserve?

Speaking freely and thinking with clarity
Opposing all oppressions
And promoting equality
Allows us to defeat
All repressions and suppressions,
Ensuring that there won't be any repeat
Of any aggressions and subjugation,
So that we can have the power
To care with the reality
The way that only we see fit.

Lena Witkowska (13)
Blacon High School, Blacon

Code: Romeo Echo Tango Romeo Echo Alpha Tango

War, a deadly thing caused by the uproar in two or more countries.
Even those who don't fight in the war retry and receive religion's bounties.
Needless to say, houses get bombed,
Even if they don't know how many.
Everyone suffers even if they're fighting to save everyone.
Doing all they can, giving up their lives to war the war.
To win the war,
Or stop it.
Really just save everyone.
Even if you give your life up,
To win the war.
Reminded day after day.
Even after it's over.
All we know.
The war was won.

Harry Giles (13)
Blacon High School, Blacon

The Crisis Of Rising Prices

It's coming up to the due date for the mortgage,
Have I saved enough money?
Can I provide for my family?
I'm anxious, this is not funny.
A week passes by, it's the day before the dreaded day.
Will I have enough to pay for my house
That I have loved since the first day.
Oh no, I am low on food,
I have to go to Tesco in my car.
I look at how much petrol I have in my tank, only 10%.
Oh no, my mortgage money is going to be lower.
This is a crisis,
The crisis of rising prices.

William Buckley (13)
Blacon High School, Blacon

The Perfect Body

She sits up at night wondering when she will be pretty.
She sits up at night wondering when she will have the
perfect body.
She sits up at night waiting for a wish to come true.
She sits up at night hoping her thighs will shrink too.
She sits up at night wishing her belly fat will be gone.
She sits up at night hoping a diet will slim her down.
She sits up at night wondering when she will be skinny.

Why? Because she thinks she's not enough for society.

Ella Blythin (13)
Blacon High School, Blacon

Liverpool Poem

They are everything we dream
Liverpool is not just a team
They are forever in our sight
All day and all night
It's a team we forever adore
Win, lose or draw
A team that makes me proud
To speak out loud
Is only ever one choice
But forever in our voice
Top 4, the title or a trophy
What may come to be
2022 has just begun
2021 has since gone.

Harry Bennion (13)
Blacon High School, Blacon

Engineering

I aspire to be an engineer so I can build what I want.
Learning more about engineering.
I will need to go to college or university to study and work hard.

E xpert
N oise
G raphics
I nspired
N otes
E lements
E xtra parts
R espect
I nstructions
N ew
G lasses/goggles.

Ethan Thompson (11)
Blacon High School, Blacon

Pandemic

P laying with friends has stopped.
A t the moment I am feeling so bored.
N ot allowed to go out longer than an hour.
D oing work at home.
E veryone's scared of falling ill.
M y mum's going mad.
I solation, I can't cope, I'm losing my mind.
C an't wait for this to end.

Henrietta Jones (11)
Blacon High School, Blacon

Cold War Poverty

When the Cold War starts
Between two hearts,
They found fault
In every word,
They burn the bridge
And dig the ditch
And build the fort
And slam the doors
And smash the plates
And close the gates
And draw the lines
And scream and cry.
This war is no good,
Both hearts get wounded.

George Thomas Davies (13)
Blacon High School, Blacon

Animals

On top of a mountain
Or under the sea,
There are so many places
Where creatures may be.
Alone in a desert
Or grouped on the farm
Or tucked in a tree trunk,
Away from all harm.
On bright, sunny grasslands
Or in a dark cave.
In jungles and forest
We all must be brave.

Molly Robinson (13)
Blacon High School, Blacon

Reedie

Reedie is life
Reedie is love
Reedie's my world
Reedie is God
Reedie is my soul
Reedie is the man
He had a plan to save Planet Earth
But then he got banged by Archie Henney
Now we are sad
But hopefully he has a speedy recovery
And gets better and comes back stronger.

Harry Kidd (13)
Blacon High School, Blacon

I Love Tesco

T he love it gives me is great.

E xcellent.

S omething like the excitement it gives me is a shock.

C ome here for a meal deal.

O vercome with sadness when my favourite meal deal isn't there.

Bailey Barlow (11)

Blacon High School, Blacon

How To Stop War?

War, do we need it?
Stop the war
People are dying
Lives are wrecked
You're destroying the world
Let people live their lives in peace
Let nature and life be
End war.

Alex Crimes (13)
Blacon High School, Blacon

Social Media Can Be Good Or Bad

Social media can be good
But sometimes it can be bad for you
If you text someone they might take it the wrong way
I'd rather be with my friend than text them or call them.

Jess Jones (11)
Blacon High School, Blacon

Lou The One-Eyed Pug

Loud and energetic pug
That likes to give hugs.
She likes when you rub her belly
But she is very smelly.
She has one eye
And sticks out her tongue all the time.

Layla Coldrick (13)
Blacon High School, Blacon

Earth = Home

Ignorance
Ignorance dwells in
The mind of humanity.
For an example, look no further.
80 bags discovered in one whale,
Shipped out to the ocean as if it were mail.
This continues to occur,
A never-before-seen wave of pollution.
Recorded, we now have proof
Of this apparent 'spoof'.
And we still
Continue to ignore,
Despite the fact
We have a solution.

Hope
Hope dwells in
The mind of humanity.
Look no further,
Than the guy next to you,
The girl across the street,
The man who's just so sweet.
Look no further than
The good of people.

Nairn Mitchell (14)
Braeview Academy, Dundee

Freedom

She told me to be free
Free me, see me, jump, jump out of the water
Look at me, I am free
I will jump from these waves and scream, "Wheee!"

The city next to the sea towers over me
I will see where the waves take me
Take me north, no, take me south, no
Take me to the tropical beaches of Hawaii.

The sights of the sky
Make me feel like I can fly
I stare at the blue, blue sea ahead of me
I can see the journey ahead of me.

What is that I see?
Oh, it's the tropical beaches of Hawaii
Where have they gone?
No, not the tropical beaches of Hawaii
There's still a journey ahead of me.

What is that? It's a fellow in the sea
Or a killer who is free
Whichever it is, I would rather be free
But I could have some company
We will see.

I will try to see if they will keep me company
On second thoughts, what if it's a killer in the sea?
I will continue on my journey
Let's see what's ahead of me.

I see the sea
On the horizon, is that a sign to be free
Or is it the sunny beaches of Hawaii?
Let's push on and see.

I see, I see
The sunny beaches of Hawaii
Go, go to the clear water of the sea
Swim, swim with the creatures that adore me
This is where I see the beauty of the sea
I have finally made it to the place where I am free.

Dawid Wloch (14)
Braeview Academy, Dundee

Ocean Pollution

The ocean is getting polluted,
Fish are dying, creatures are becoming extinct,
Coral reefs are dying due to climate change.
Turtles are mistaking plastic bags for jellyfish
And are suffocating to death on them.
Whales eat microplastics when they try to eat plankton.
Cargo vessels interrupt whales' migrations to places with
more food.

The
icebergs
are melting away.
Penguins are losing their habitats,
walruses are losing resting places because all
of the ice is melting. Polar bears are struggling to
find food and their cubs and the mother will starve with
climate change melting the ice. Animals are losing their
homes, food and lives. As plastic use increases, the more our
oceans get polluted by microplastics.
More animals die, more ecosystems die.
Fish and other aquatic sea life become endangered.
Ice caps melt and crack, falling into the freezing ocean,
crushing sea animals, flattening homes.
Turtles choke on plastic bags, fish get tangled in fishing
nets, fishermen are overfishing and killing exotic creatures.
Whales are eating bags and microplastics.
Stop creating single-use plastics.

Save the creatures.
Save the oceans.

Jamie Minto (14)
Braeview Academy, Dundee

Life Of A Tree

Colourful
    Relaxing
    Calm
      Glistening
      Glittery
     Bright
       Crystal-clear
        Light like passion
       Lonely
        Damaged
         Uncared for
         Dirty seas
         Struck
         Nowhere to go
       Polar bears
     Extinct?
    No more
   Life
  Ice gone
 Ice melting
Shocking
Before and after
Bright to dull
Habitable
Beautiful to ugly

Death
Dying
Planet Plastic
Or
Planet Earth?
Help
Help others
Help the planet
Because we can!

Ellis Milne (14)

Braeview Academy, Dundee

Tribute To A Leaf

It's autumn.
The crisp morning air all around.
I fumble.
Off my branch, I'm on the ground.
The wind blows.
I'm on my way...
Off the pier, I fly, over the water.
I drift,
    I drift,
        I stop.
            I land.
A plastic bottle.
The plastic bottle I lay upon.
Why would there be such plastic in the ocean?
On this bottle I lay upon, I float.
Days.
    Weeks.
        Months.
            Years.
How has the bottle I lay upon not disappeared?
Why does this ocean feel so crowded?
I see bottles,
        I see packets,
                I see rubbish.

I begin to wonder,
Is this plastic or planet?

Ava Means (14)
Braeview Academy, Dundee

Instead Of Planet

Bed not made
Not ready for the day
Crumpled up uniform

Prison-looking
Not appealing

Sketchy scene
Junkies

Jam-packed bins
Making streets manky

Dirty, polluted water
Icebergs melting

The happy and colourful coral
Turns into sad and depressing coral.

We need to bin our litter
It's killing wildlife

There's so much plastic in the world
We should start calling it Plastic Earth
Instead of Planet

We are letting other countries rot
As we keep shipping waste to them

This is our doing
We can stop *now!*

Bin litter
Before things get bitter.

Mathew Brady (14)

Braeview Academy, Dundee

Trees

Trees make oxygen.
Trees take carbon dioxide.
But we are destroying those trees.

Paper is being made.
Paper is being wasted.
More trees are falling down.

Trees that make oxygen.
Trees that take carbon dioxide.
We are destroying those trees.

Paper is being made
From trees that make oxygen.
Paper is being wasted
So we cut down more trees.

Trees that make oxygen
That take carbon dioxide.

Paper is being made from
Trees
Trees
Trees.

Alex Thoms (14)
Braeview Academy, Dundee

The Beast

Lurking around the waters,
Prowling for its next victim.
A deadly killer,
Striking time and time again,
Wiping out many, many creatures.
Avoid at all costs.
It camouflages,
Hides,
Waiting.
But this creature doesn't sting,
Nor bite.
It wraps itself around its prey,
Suffocating, choking,
Killing.
It rules the waters,
On the surface,
Or in the depths.
It looks harmless,
But don't be fooled.

This dangerous beast
Is called Plastic.

Alicia Curran (14)
Braeview Academy, Dundee

Untold

The water bashes into the sand
The clash, the contrast, the shift
Deep beneath the water
Colourful coral colonies buzz

Unknowing fish wander the depths...
Naive.
Naive.
Naive.
Horrors thrive in the depths...

Crashing through the waves, they chase
Chomping through the flesh.

Echoes
Echoes of the horror
Stories yet to be told
Fables tangled in the seaweed
Legends left behind.

Ryan Weir (14)
Braeview Academy, Dundee

How To See The World

Destroyed, lonely, disgusting,
Calm, reflective, glistening,
Rotting, bland, dim,
Warm, beautiful, healthy.

Boring, colourless, unhealthy,
Shocking, suffocating, melting,
Dim, toxic, gone,
Talking, smug, cold.

Chilling, crucial, crisis,
Unhelpful, useless, infested,
Poor state, unclean and the 'loophole',
Which is dumping waste abroad.

This is our planet and our leaders.

Ava Finnon (13)
Braeview Academy, Dundee

Plastic

Polluted with it,
Suffocated by it,
Trapped by it,
Soon, we will be made of it,
Even born with it,
But *we* are the reason
We're polluted with it,
Suffocated by it,
Trapped by it.

Lily Mitchell (13)
Braeview Academy, Dundee

Life's Lie And Death's Truth

Heroes follow life while villains head down.
Heroes follow life for hours, while villains head for death since the beginning.
I got told to stand in the cold.
But I gave you a warning.
That the heat you bring, will bring you defeat.
Life and death are the same in fear.
But are different due to ways you die.
People fear death because of how many gruesome ways life expels you from it.
But people choose to die because they understand what they should know.
To pray that there are reasons to live and to die.
It's your choice but before you take a side.
Prove it's the right side and not the wrong.
Many regret choices they made in life
Soon that came back, ghosts come back to reincarnate their mistakes.
So make the most you can.
Because life is short, but death is not.

Eliza Igo (13)

Copley Academy, Stalybridge

He

"I'm a he, not a she!" I scream!
He, he, he!
I cry asking why it is me who is she.
I cut my hair with care.
I need to be he!
I change my name, hoping for slight fame.
I walk into school feeling not that cool.
I get stares and I get scared.
On my shoulder I feel a tap,
It's my friend with his dirty cap.
He hates me.
He gasps for air and gives me a stare.
"You are a she, not a he!"
He runs.
I cry and ask why I was born a she.
During class the teacher says my name.
She thinks it's lame and everyone laughs.
Now it's lunch, I drink my fruit punch.
I am alone.
I go home and cry in my bed.
I ask in my head,
Why am I she and not he?
I hear a knock, it's my mum.
She is cuddling me.
"To me you are a he."

I smile. "I am a he?"
She says yes and I am sad less.
I go to school the day after.
All I hear is laughter.
I move school so I feel better.
I go and they give me a letter.
'We support you' on the letter it says.
I feel happy like a bunch of sun rays.
We need more supporters of the community
Please treat it with respect.

Ethan Mcguinness (11)
Copley Academy, Stalybridge

A World Of Dreams

Poverty, pandemic, destruction and murder
Just some of the things that send us into disorder
The world right now is so crooked and strange
And some of its people refuse to change.
People have dreams (that's right, they do)
Everyone has dreams, even you
People have dreams that are waiting to be fulfilled,
But instead people are being weak-willed.
I have a dream to work with AI
But people will be frightened so much they will fly
"Throw them away! They will rise and destroy us one day!"
But I wish to say, "Calm down, chill out!
If they do rise up it's our fault for bringing them about!"

Archie Taylor (11)
Copley Academy, Stalybridge

Women

W omen are strong, powerful people, and deserve to be equal to men

O ver a long period of time, many fearless and independent women fought for freedom and the right for speech for women, like Sojourner Truth who fought for gender and racial equality and Simone de Beavoir who paved the way for modern feminism.

M en are not superior to women and should never be.

E veryone should be treated as equals, no one has superiority!

N o woman should feel as if she is inferior, worthless, or has no self value, as women are strong, independent and powerful people who have a history that makes us unique and stronger people.

Brooke Dickson (13)
Copley Academy, Stalybridge

Our Dark Future...

Dark skies fill the lands,
the air foul with decay.
Factory chimneys burning constantly,
fumes start to sway.
Death, destruction and pollution,
cover up our once blue seas,
flowers rattling and dying,
leaving no purpose for bees.
Deforestation destroying trees,
young children cracking cocoa beans,
people put to work in factories before
they're even teens.
High levels of radiation,
leaves shadows left behind,
there is only one solution to this,
that we really need to find.
So let's make a change just to save our world.
So please,
let this poem be heard.

Isaac John Matthews (11)
Copley Academy, Stalybridge

My Dogs

Although I have five goofy, loveable dogs
Alena always comes first.
She's so caring and gentle towards anyone she comes
across.
She deserves all the treats in the world.
She loves to cuddle and play like a little puppy
She's so fluffy, cuddly and silly.
Alena this is for you.
People think dogs are just animals
But they're really not.
People who own them put all their love and trust into them
They're like your own child and they're so protective.
When they pass away it's the saddest most terrible moment
in your lifetime
It's like everything has just left you.

Gracie-Leigh Mann (11)
Copley Academy, Stalybridge

To Bark

Dogs bark to mark
That they have lived and they do continue to.

I think in this way we all bark,
We want to be remembered.
For as long as our memories last,
Far into the past.
You see,
Writing and drawing,
Painting and singing,
Smiling and dancing.

All to show the same thing,
That they danced and sang,
Loved and liked,
Cried and grieved,
Took and lent,
Came and went,
And lived like us.

We have all lived and live we do,
But isn't it funny we spend it
Spend that time we have living
Proving that we have?

Tia Hadfield (13)
Copley Academy, Stalybridge

Death In The Air

It is 1942 on the border of Germany,
Five squadrons of B17s and Lancaster bombers
Cover the sky like a flock of birds,
They are escorted by Spitfires and P51s,
When they get closer into the heart of Germany,
The British and American pilots feel anxious,
Waiting for the ambush to happen,
The flack begins,
The Germans unleash their deadly wrath on the British,
The nimble Spitfires and P51s swoop into action,
Attacking the enemy,
The Lancasters drop their payload on the land below,
Destroying their targets,
Mission complete!
Coming home with a victory.

Jack Yates (11)
Copley Academy, Stalybridge

Today Not Tomorrow

Today not tomorrow
Today not tomorrow
The girls are being suffocated in the fact
They may not be allowed to get the jobs they want
Because of what people think.

Today not tomorrow
Today not tomorrow
The colour pink is still interpreted to be a 'girly' colour
Dresses and skirts are still 'girly'
And tracksuits are for 'boys'.

Today not tomorrow
Today not tomorrow
Young girls are growing
Thinking they cannot be a builder or doctor or technician

Today not tomorrow.

Jaimee Platt (12)
Copley Academy, Stalybridge

Animals' Environments

Animals' homes are being taken down but
It's not too late to save them
To stop this from happening we need to stop deforestation
Because we really don't need to do that
Stop killing animals for the sake of it
Deforestation is a big thing that needs to stop
We need to treat their environment the same way we want
ours to go
It's not okay!
So at the end of the day don't say, "Hey it's alright, the trees
will grow back"
What, so you can do it again?
No!

Rubyann Burrows (11)
Copley Academy, Stalybridge

It's Our Responsibility

The world is slowly dying
Dying ever so slow
By destroying trees that go to waste
With some random doodles
People even waste delicious noodles
Plants are rotting and losing their colour
Some people don't have enough money for butter
Octopuses are drying up
Getting washed up on shores
Soon they'll go extinct and we won't have any more
Show respect to this planet
But if you don't, you'll regret it
Please save the world
Before it's too late.

Jodie Green (12)
Copley Academy, Stalybridge

We Have Something To Say

It's been too long and I have something to say,
Stop deforestation before it's too late,
Stop using the environment to get your way,
Stop saying it will all be okay,
We need to save our trees and all of their leaves,
When it's too late we can't get up and leave,
We only have one Earth and one life,
We need to use them right,
We are the future,
It's all in our hands,
It's up to us and the generations before us,
The next generation is counting on us.

Eva Milhench (11)
Copley Academy, Stalybridge

Humans Are Strange

Humans are strange
They build and prosper
Only to blow it all away

Humans are strange
They act like they like you
But then they just lead you astray

Humans are strange
They say "Be yourself"
Then shun those who do just that

Humans are strange
They preach love and care
But then it just goes at the drop of a hat.

Humans are strange
And I truly can't believe
That I am human, too.

Isabelle Fisher-Gould (12)
Copley Academy, Stalybridge

My Dream

Acting and musicals are everything to me
I like singing and dancing
I'm good at dancing
I love musicals, they're funny
My dream is to be on stage
One day to be the star of the show
My mum and nan started my passion
taking me to Grease the musical
I've watched lots, now I'm on my way
I'm persuing my dream, getting a role in my dream show
Even though I'm not Dodger, just part of the workhouse
I'm in Oliver.

Brooke Tracey (11)
Copley Academy, Stalybridge

Everyone's Different

Everyone's different
That's how it is
You can't change someone
Because of their personality
That's how it is
Don't change yourself because
Some don't like you
Everyone's different
That's how it is
Be yourself then
You will see who you are
Everyone's different
That's how it is
Don't judge someone
Based on their colour
Because they are all people
Like you and me.

Amanta Elizabath (13)
Copley Academy, Stalybridge

Family

Family
It is everything, no matter what
They will be with you
Through your ups and downs

Family
They may seem mad
But they are not
They love you no matter what

Family
Old and young, new members join
And some leave to a better place
But they will still be in your heart.

Family
It can be torn apart
And there might be someone new
And they're your new family
They love you just the same.

Tia Holding (11)
Copley Academy, Stalybridge

The World Of Sports

Why do people love sports you may ask
Well let's start with football
You might call football boring
Because all you do is kick a ball around a field
But it's a lot more than that
Football is a passion
A sport we love to play
But if you don't play it might go away
Hobbies gone as well as jobs
But then poverty can corrupt
It would kill and hurt players
So that's why you need to watch.

Zack Ryan
Copley Academy, Stalybridge

Christmas

C hristmas is right around the corner
H earing Santa's bells in the night sky
R eading Christmas stories with our loved ones
I cicles dripping from your window
S now falling when you wake up
T reats spread under the Christmas tree
M assive piles of presents
A sleep in your bed ready for Santa to bring your presents
S inging carols round the Christmas tree.

Phoebe Payton (11)
Copley Academy, Stalybridge

Our Future

I believe that, in the future,
Most animals will be extinct.
That crocodiles, lions, sharks and even tigers
Will be no more.
I think it is time for change.
In the future there may be flying cars and trips to Mars
But at what cost?
Polluted air, deforestation, global warming? Extinction!
The future will be messed up
The scent of death in the air
No places to stay due to overpopulation.

Ruby Leckey (11)
Copley Academy, Stalybridge

A Scary Night

H ouse is dark, not a thing to be seen
A ll of a sudden something fell off the side
L oudness starts
L illy wakes everyone up
O ut of nowhere a loud bang!
W here is that coming from?
E verywhere goes silent again
E veryone hides
N ot a thing to be heard again...

Maddison Bowden (11)
Copley Academy, Stalybridge

Our World

W e all live in the same place together on Earth
O ur people can be nice, kind or sometimes discriminate
R eligions, beliefs, we are all different people
L ove is important, we should all feel it in some way
D ay by day we are all improving our skills, our thoughts
and our wellbeing.

Luke Walker (13)
Copley Academy, Stalybridge

Halloween Night

Today's the day that the ghosts and ghouls come out to
play
Kids running around in spooky costume
For tonight is Halloween night
And let me tell you, you're in for a fright
Long-haired werewolves
Blood-sucking vampires
Long-legged freaks
And they all like the taste of human meat.

Jack Fernley (11)
Copley Academy, Stalybridge

In Their Paws

No one cares, no one dares
To stop this life of death
Because no one dares to fight the lords
The world will die if no one cares
People just tread on things and destroy old buildings
And don't think of destroying our homes
They shoot us then stuff us
Why oh why do humans hate us?

Arlo Woodman (12)
Copley Academy, Stalybridge

Environment

    E nvironmental issues
    N ature
Ri **V** ers and oceans
Cl **I** mate change
 O **R** ganic
 P **O** llution
    N urture
Ani **M** als are endangered
 Gr **E** ta Thunberg fights for change
La **N** d
    T rees.

Megan Seager (12)

Copley Academy, Stalybridge

Football

Football is an amazing sport
And many people love the sport,
But others don't.
I started the sport over three years ago
And have since then never stopped playing.
People should try it.

Zachary Hafford (11)
Copley Academy, Stalybridge

Football

F reedom
O utfield fun
O ver the moon scoring
T rying
B all
A bility
L eague
L ads and girls.

Nathan Wilson (13)
Copley Academy, Stalybridge

Autumn

Orange, red and brown
What is this all about?
Leaves are falling to the ground
Something weird is happening all around
I have the sense that something is arriving
Is it an invasion, is something attacking?
Maybe it's a party, let's start dancing!

I know... autumn is starting!
The leaves are floating, the fog is coming
The wood's splendour is shining
A nature transformation
A magical creation
In September, October and November
Sadly it will end in December

And this is how autumn is
Full of falling leaves
And magical trees
And this is how we end...
Autumn, I will like to see you again.

Valeria Munoz Yeregui (12)
Harrogate Ladies' College, Harrogate

Be Aware

Plastic bottles and charred glass
Ripped-up newspaper lying on the grass
Stop tearing up all of the forest's trees
Is this what we want for you and me?

Blue skies up high no longer clear
The air we fill with smoke and death
Do we stand up for the future children's fear?
Ourselves we hurt for no breath

Crystal clear our waters gleamed
Fish-abundant rivers streamed
Ocean floors, sandy white
Now littered with all this fright

What are we going to do to stop the world from disease?
Our waters, skies, wildlife and trees
They are all at risk if we do not act now!

Scarlett Wright (12)
Harrogate Ladies' College, Harrogate

Our Future

O ver the dappled moors and round the river bend

U pon the crisp soil and under the sapphire spring sky

R oses, erigeron, foxglove and sweetpeas lie so peacefully, not wanting to say goodbye

F ast forward fifty years and look at our Earth

U pon the intoxicated soil and round the billowing smoke

T oo disfigured to call our Earth, too broken to call a home

U nder the blacking smog draped across the world

R ight is not done enough, wrong is just easier

E very day you ignore this, our Earth will break down. Choose your future, the world is in your hands.

Rose Smalley (12)
Harrogate Ladies' College, Harrogate

Losing Someone

To lose someone is like losing your heart,
It feels missing and broken and like it will shatter apart,
You feel like you will never feel seen,
But all you need is time to feel alive,
If you live through this moment then you can survive,
All you need is someone to help,
Someone that makes you happy and feel like yourself,
Sometimes losing someone can play with your mind,
But all you need is someone nice and kind,
Eventually that hole in your heart will fade away,
You will still miss them but not every day,
Do not focus on the hardships of life,
Focus on happiness and that will suffice.

Poppy Bo Man (12)
Harrogate Ladies' College, Harrogate

Trust

Everyone trusts nature,
Every plant and every creature.
The sun's shining rays,
And all those rainy days.
We trust it to be there,
For our every care.

But what if nature doesn't trust us?
With every single bus,
Emitting its gas,
Maybe nature wants to pass.
All the littered plastic,
Do our actions need to be more drastic?

Your words have power,
With every minute of every hour,
Nature, like kelp,
Will perish from our lack of help.
Now let me get this straight,
Nature needs to put its trust in us, it can't wait.

Isabel Badger (12)

Harrogate Ladies' College, Harrogate

The World Is Green

The world is green
Lush and bright
Soaring high in the clear blue sky
A wild goose flight
Frolicking in the fresh soft grass
Feeling the warm breeze pass
The bonnie deer galloping in the dazzling fields
We can't protect the world with just plain shields
Words have the power to heal our land
Are you just going to lay there or are you going to stand?
We will be brave and we will fight
We will do everything we can with all our might
To save this world
And make it clean
For the plants, for the animals
Make the world green!

Lyra Javed (12)
Harrogate Ladies' College, Harrogate

Once...

There was once light amongst the darkness,
Once smiles amongst the despair,
But blatant evil is replacing the happiness,
Taking over their land without a care.
They had to leave,
They had to run.
Did anyone believe
That just one gun
Could ruin a family,
Destroy their home.
One big catastrophe,
So they were free to roam
A beautiful land,
That was not theirs,
A single strand,
That had no cares.
But they did break through,
They did bring pain,
So it's up to you,
To stand with Ukraine!

Rosie Kelly (12)
Harrogate Ladies' College, Harrogate

Life

Life comes and goes,
It's short or lengthy.
Life is hard,
But no need to be in a frenzy.

Nursery, primary school, high school,
Fourteen years of learning.
School is tiring and hard,
But in the end it's worth it.

Later in your life,
You start to get a job.
Now a family you love,
Life is no more a blob.

When getting near the end,
Spend time with those you adore.
Life is not awfully long,
Before you're stuck in the trapdoor.

Jasmin Rhodes (13)
Harrogate Ladies' College, Harrogate

Falling And Flying

I fall to the ground,
I have no hope,
I'm crying oceans full of tears,
I opened my heart,
And it got broken,
I'm thinking the unthinkable,
That I could get up,
Start a new life,
A new hope,
A new future,
After falling to the ground,
I catch myself,
And start again,
With a new perspective,
A new life,
A new future.

Florence Coyle (12)
Harrogate Ladies' College, Harrogate

Peer Pressure

I'm out with my friends, we're having a blast
But time seems to be ticking just too fast
We walk up the road where the corner shops lie
They've got a fake ID and they want to get high
I refuse and refuse, but nothing works
They say I'm just a baby and they all smirk.

Am I in the wrong? Am I just a baby?
They must all think I'm that, I'm crazy
They walk into the shop acting all weird
My best friend just looked at me and sneered
Their plan worked, they got the drugs
I thought they were my friends, not wasted thugs.

They wave the drugs in the air
As I look at them with despair
"Have some," they all cheered
But this is what I feared
I throw the drugs and stand my ground,
After doing that I felt so proud
"We won't be your friends if you don't have any,"
they claimed
But if we get caught I don't want to be blamed
As I grab the drugs, I look at them with disgrace
With a single tear dripping down my face...

Natalia Creese (12)
Holmer Green Senior School, Holmer Green

A Day As A Poppy

A day as a poppy, is all I want,
A day as a poppy would make my day bloom,
Every time we hear gunshots fire,
My heart starts racing like it's on fire,
Not many of us left, not many at all.
All trampled like garden tools.
A day as a poppy would mean the world to me,
A day as poppy, what a day it could be.
Once again, I hear guns, guns fire, guns fire indeed.
A day as a poppy, a day indeed,
A day as a poppy would make my world complete,
A day as a poppy, a day indeed,
What a day it could be.
Just me, just me alone, sat on the field,
With no one to hold, as quiet as it can be,
All guns on hold, this Christmas Eve.
They're back again, they're back indeed,
To crush us once more, to crush us beneath their feet.

What a month it has been, what a month indeed,
What will life bring? Life indeed.
What could have been is no longer seen,
Thought to have been demolished,
Demolished into nothing that's seen.

Forced, forced to hide, forced to hide indeed,
Hide from the outside, the outside indeed.

What's seen is now gone, what's gone is now seen,
The world's turned upside down, upside down indeed.

My life is at its end, its end indeed,
What a life it has been, what a life indeed,
So many things I wanted to do,
So many things I regret,
My life was nice, it was nice indeed,
So peaceful yet eventful, eventful indeed.

Quiet at last, as quiet as can be,
I loved my life as my life loved me.
I say goodbye, this is goodbye indeed.

Ivy-Rose Gleeson (11)
Holmer Green Senior School, Holmer Green

Different

I open my eyes and I can see
The person that I want to be
I know what I am and I'm ready
Ready to be someone
Someone who
Someone who is listened to

I know I'm not the same
Maybe it's my name
But I know who I am
Don't try to say
That I'm different every other day

I am who I am and it will never change
Don't make me think that I am strange
This is me
And I am free
To be exactly what I want to be

I've looked left and right
But I'm not wrong
Who should care if I clap or sing a song?

The world must change before it ends
We need to welcome those brave enough
When that day comes, that they talk about them

Because I am different and I can see
The person that I want to be
And that's why I'm different
All of you know it
Don't give me weird looks when I try to show it

You can't say that we are all the same
Because of our flaws or because of our fame
But you should know that there is no shame
When you stand up and say what you want to say
Any night or any day

We aren't good but we're not that bad
We're only human but that's no reason to be sad
Because every single person is different
You know it, I know it
It's okay to show it
It's who we are
It's what we say
It is what we do every day
That is why we aren't the same
And that is why we all matter
If you're happy or sad, or mad as a hatter

This is who we are
We are different
I am different

Different
Different
Different.

Freddie Phillips (12)
Holmer Green Senior School, Holmer Green

Thank You, Lord

Thank you, Lord, for food and water
Thank you, Lord, for watching over us
Thank you, Lord, for taking care of our loved ones
Thank you, Lord, for trying the most you can to help Ukraine
Thank you, Lord, for loving us as much as we love you
Thank you, Lord, for watching every single one to make sure
bad does not come to you
Thank you, Lord, for always being next to us even in the
darkest moments

The Lord is with us no matter what
He will always protect you
Never lose hope even in the darkest moments
But shall not think he will always help you
As the Lord helps good and shall not stand for evil
Jesus as well will only help the good
They both are caring with full hearts
They will never leave your side
Not even when you think your life is doomed
There standing next to you facing it as well
You're never alone

Now you may be wondering what the message is
Well that is to never lose hope in the Lord
He is with you forever
Amen.

Jacob Goldsmith (11)
Holmer Green Senior School, Holmer Green

I Am Not Your Doll

I am not your doll
So do not treat me as such
Do not ever tell me I do not deserve as much
You plait my hair, you dress me up
You want me to wash your dishes and cups
You tell me I'm not good enough, that I am too big or too small
That I always think too much, or that I'm much too tall
I must always dress to please but never show too much
Because if I do get hurt, I encouraged them to touch
I am not your doll!

I am not your doll
I am not here to conform
But if I don't, I am ousted because I do not fit in with the norm
You put blush on my cheek
And make me appear weak
You squeeze me into outfits that you think I should wear
And do what you want to do, with my own goddam hair
I'm fed up with being told
That in order to win the gold
I must listen to you because that's not fair
I am not your doll!

I am not your doll
My actions are not yours to control
I refuse to go on like this, just doing what I'm told
You do not control me
Like a bird, I am free
So go on and try to hold me down
I do not fear you, you stupid clown
I will do as I wish when I wish to do it
Because you do not control me, you utter and complete twit!
I am not your doll.

Lola Harris (12)

Holmer Green Senior School, Holmer Green

You Are Awesome, Keep It That Way

You are awesome no matter what you say.
You are awesome every single day.
Don't doubt yourself if other people doubt you.
You are awesome, keep it that way.
Every day when the sun rises keep your head up.
Do the best you can.
You are awesome in your own way.
Every night as the moon comes out repeat, you
are awesome
And keep it with you.
If you fail try again, don't give up, there will be success.
If you lose a race no need to pout, try again until you win.
You are awesome.
If you sit there and cry there will be no success, you are
awesome every single day.
Try and try, you are the best you are,
Don't copy your friends, you're unique in your own way.
Every day you step into school you are awesome, and it will
never change.
If you love your parents and they love, you keep it with you.
You are awesome in your way.
This poem is done, and you have your message.
Remember you are awesome every single day.

Owen Turner (11)
Holmer Green Senior School, Holmer Green

Diversity

Black and white, that's all they see
Why can't the colours merge and let them be free?
Why do we have to be apart?
Don't you know everyone has a heart?

How did we deserve the throne?
We may not have the same skin colour but we are all made
from bone
Why did our ancestors take them from their home?
No longer will we make them feel alone

Why did we make them pick cotton
Making them live a life which is unfair and rotten?
Why can't we join as one
A society that is inclusive and involves everyone?

The Earth is a planet for all
Not a place where there is hatred and a constant brawl
Let's end all the dictatorship and war
See people for not what they look like, but who they are
from the core

So let's all hold hands, stand up and fight
Let diversity shine like a beautiful bright light.

Jenna Kerr (13)
Holmer Green Senior School, Holmer Green

Consequence

Every day glaciers fall into the ocean
All of this is leaving us broken
So much majestic wildlife left without a home
Poor little cubs left all alone
This is global warming; this is our consequence

Our seasons slowly drifting away
It makes us think, will we see another day?
Soon there will be no November
Do they remember?
This is global warming; this is our consequence

Oceans are rising
See all the lightning and thunder?
This really makes us wonder
How long do we have until we are all under?
This is global warming; this is our consequence

So many wildfires soaring away
Is this really the right way?
Losing all of Earth's gorgeousness
We are not using our cautiousness
This is global warming, this is our consequence

However, there is still hope
We need to get off this downward slope
Our world is hanging by a thread
But all we need to do is to look ahead
This is our home, we need to save it.

Charlie Vittle (12)
Holmer Green Senior School, Holmer Green

The Fire Always Burns

The fire always burns within us to save our world for
generations,
If we all work together this will burn across the nation,
The ice is melting, what are we going to do?
Climate change is already here, it's time to make our debut.

The seas are rising,
The sun is shining,
Where are the polar bears going to live?
To save our world isn't an option, it's something we have to
give.

Climate change is not a segment of your imagination,
Try to help out instead of playing the PlayStation,
Seeing the ice melt fills me with the vexation,
Climate change is killing our world like an assassination.

Stop burning fossil fuels,
Global warming is a battle and we are losing the duel,
We have to get our act together and save our world,
Or even the god Hades can't send us to the Underworld.

Yusuf Shaker (12)
Holmer Green Senior School, Holmer Green

Expectations

Staring at yourself in the mirror
Does your blurry face become any clearer?
You call up a surgeon
To fix all your burdens

He jabs needles in your skin left and right
Is beauty worth no appetite?
After the surgery, you're worn and tired
Was it worth it just to be admired?
The plastic in your skin feels unusual and weird
You force a smile, swallowing your fear
Your face looks distorted, odd and ugly
Was it worth almost all your money?

Can you please just tell me
Is it true that pain is beauty?
Did those expectations get to your head
To the point where your heart shattered with dread?

To all the girls who hate themselves
Who hate their nose, their stomach, their face
To all the girls who are under twelve
Love yourself, and embrace.

Heidi Neville (13)
Holmer Green Senior School, Holmer Green

A Spark Of Hope

We always have hope,
Even if things look bad
We always have hope,
The environment is dying,
We always have hope,
We have to act fast,
We always have hope,
Some people in the world are helping, we need all,
We always have hope,
Pollution, deforestation, climate change - it hurts
We always have hope,
The actions we take are proving decisive
We always have hope,
The future is dark but if we act fast everything will change
We always have hope,
For generations we have been burning fossil fuels, only now
we realise
We always have hope,
We need to change even though this sounds dull, we live in
hope
We always have hope,

This is where we change
This is where we change
At this moment, this is where we change
We always have hope.

Jamie Kearvell (12)
Holmer Green Senior School, Holmer Green

Memories

Looking back on the year so far
My memories drift to trips in the car
We head off early, we're raring to go
Car packed to the rafters from high to low
Whether it be wet weather gear or sunglasses on
It's going to be amazing
Let's make the most before the day is gone
I love a day at the beach with the sand on my toes
Or bundling up warm with a woolly hat and a cold nose
It's creating fun memories with family and friends
Like going to theme parks laughing and joking
And the texts that we send
On the long journeys home and the fun that we had
I start to feel tired
And a little bit sad
But I know that there are more
Things to enjoy and experiences
To try
Let's enjoy every moment of childhood
As time trickles by.

Jessica Lewington (13)
Holmer Green Senior School, Holmer Green

We Want Peace

It hurts so bad, feels like I've got cancer
I'm not a snow leopard, I'm a black panther
Black lives matter, I can't breathe
Peace is what we want, peace is what we need

You're crushing our souls while we protest
We're asking you people to get off our necks
It's been going on for far too long
Can't we all just get along?
You need to realise that this is wrong

I'm that blackbird in the sky
We will protest day and night
Until we succeed
Peace is what we want
Peace is what we need

After all these years of shedding tears
You need to open your ears while we're fighting our fear
To George Floyd, even though I didn't know you
You're a part of my heart
I wish I could show you how much you mean to me
And all of us want peace so give it to us.

Gabriella Ramdeen
Holmer Green Senior School, Holmer Green

Racism Is Not Needed

R acism is a form of cruelty
A ll of this is not needed
C ities under pressure
I ndividuals that are different treated harshly
S ome people getting hurt and killed
M aybe think twice about your actions

I s it necessary to be cruel?
S o many people affected

N ot everyone is the same and that's okay
O ur community is meant to be peaceful
T ime to stick together, not be torn apart

N o, you may not have experienced it but...
E ach and every one of us is affected differently
E veryone has feelings
D oes it really affect you?
E ven just speaking up would help
D o you feel the need?

Imogen Blackwell (12)
Holmer Green Senior School, Holmer Green

World Peace

Over the horizon, the sun may fall
Along with the soldiers that fought for us all
Even if it rained, they were out there too
They screamed, they shouted and even cried

But that didn't stop them, they still tried to survive
One day, they knew world peace would arrive
"You shoot me down, but I won't fall," they screamed
"I'm unstoppable today," they cried

Tears fell onto the dry, brown land
And they fought till they held their wives' hands
Everything was dark
Everything was grey

But something kept them happy
Blood-red dots flowered in November
But nothing happened in September
Luckily, memories kept them going

A year had passed
And in November
Not September
They won the war

World peace was restored.

Freya Owen
Holmer Green Senior School, Holmer Green

Peer Pressure

P eer pressure is not okay,

E verything could go wrong,

E ven if it was a 'joke',

R ealising you could ruin someone's day from that one 'joke'

P raying you didn't hurt them the same night,

R anting to your friends how it was 'funny' seeing them cry

E va got sent to hospital because she tried drugs,

S omeone said to her, "Try this sweet," now her immune system is failing,

S eeing her in hospital made people cry,

U ntil everything was okay and she was back in school,

R eally be careful with the words you say and the actions you use,

E verything could go wrong.

Reece Herbst (11)
Holmer Green Senior School, Holmer Green

Doubt

Doubt
Crawling up your back
Striking when you least expect it
Striking when you slack
Even when you say, "It's okay"
There's always a little voice in your head
Making you dread
Doubt

But even if you fear the worst
You're going to be alright
Because people are around you
They're all there to help you
All you need is a big warm hug
And some coffee in your mug
Wrapped up tight in your blanket

You're going to be alright
Because your future is bright
Surrounded by your loved ones
You'll see doubt will soon be gone
Locked up tight
Letting out the light
You're going to be alright.

Georgia Spinks-Gillen (14)

Holmer Green Senior School, Holmer Green

The Cost Of Living

I n this world the cost of living strikes us all down

N ever let yourself fall to it; get up and fight it

S adness corrupts all who give up fighting

P ress on forward and show the world what you can do

I f you fail then try, try again until you succeed

R ushing through life only costs you more

A ny attempt to corrupt your happiness, fight back and enjoy yourself

T he cost of living strikes us down; just stand up and shake it off

I f society denies anything you say, just stay happy

O ppressing the sadness never works

N ever give up; follow your dreams and the cost of life will disappear.

Harry Ratcliffe (12)

Holmer Green Senior School, Holmer Green

Environment

World spinning upside down
World spinning all around
That smell of pollution
Knowing we need a solution
And it all comes down to this

That little penguin all alone
Floating on some cracked bone
A swim in the sea
Is constantly surrounded by the packaging of Maccy Ds
And it all comes down to this

The fresh morning air is now filled with fumes
And it takes away from the smell of my neighbours' blooms
A monkey comes to steal the dames
Because his home is up in flames
And it all comes down to this

But maybe
Maybe we can just share that ride with Suzie
So Mum doesn't feel so floozie
And not buying that plastic one that is a bit shifty
But instead of that metal one that is an extra 4.50.

Lily Dell (12)
Holmer Green Senior School, Holmer Green

Growing Up

The days that came after that phase of crawling,
The nights of frights and years of yawning,
The day comes when all those years of crawling have just been done,
And now there's no other way but walking.

Days may come when you think life is slow,
But after a while you'll suddenly see that life is precious and you've not got long to go.
Some days may come, some weeks will go,
But trust me your life isn't that slow.

Years will go and you will look back and think oh damn why can't life just be slow!
You may want to be an adult but when you're older you'll look back and think, why did I want that?

Ava Spencer (11)

Holmer Green Senior School, Holmer Green

Anxiety

Sitting in light, only seeing the dark
Acting confident to try to make my mark
Teenage girls
Anxiety
Am I good enough?

Lying down, crying myself to sleep
Three-year-old me knew I wasn't this weak
The boys and girls who call me names
Do they feel no shame?

The hot summer left like ice
A bit of comfort, wouldn't that be nice?
Feeling old and torn, you made me new
Now I stand with the scars of what you put me through

My worst habit is my own sadness
Left in solitude and a mess
Mind is grey and heavy and full
Thoughts pointless, unnecessary and dull

So, as the seasons change
I'm learning to be brave
Not everything in life goes my way
But I say I'm fine and walk away.

Elisabeth Last (12)
Holmer Green Senior School, Holmer Green

How The World Will Change

This is a question I ask a lot
How will the world change?
We will find out when the time is right
When I'm twenty, where will I be?
I've got the world ahead of me, what will I be?
I might own a business, or be a Christmas elf
Or maybe, just maybe, I could be a mountain climber
That climbs higher than Edmund Hillary himself
Everything is changing second after second
When I am older, the world will be different
Flying cars? We will find out.
It's mad to think this is not it, everything will be different
Nothing will ever stay the same
We all know the future will come
It's a rollercoaster we're queuing for
It is going to be great!

Charlie Pisani (11)
Holmer Green Senior School, Holmer Green

Environment

Why are we making the world fall to the ground
and why are we doing nothing about it?
Why doesn't anyone care?
Because we should care
Every single one of us should care
Because this world matters, this world matters so much
It matters more than me and you
So, before you litre or before you drive a car
And all the pollution comes out into the world
Think... *do I need to drive or can I walk?*
Do I need to litre or should I walk?
For a couple of minutes or even a couple of seconds
To just put it in the bin
Because if you want to live on this planet
We have to look after it.

Harry Edwards
Holmer Green Senior School, Holmer Green

Weather

Mount Ararat spun dark stones
Grey shadows lifted inside the ark
The palm trees dancing
In the wind
Pink dawn awakened animals
White doves soar in the air
I saw green leaves flutter and fall

The water running down the mountain
The water trickling
And the birds chirping
While the sun sets

Thunder blankets, waterfall cascades
The eroding cliff being destroyed by water
Down in the wooden belly, we sang songs
Lifted hands, cried, laughed and slept
Waited for Genesis sign to unfold
Moonlight

Upper deck, He whispered, "Noah"
The star trails
Sunlight on land and halos appear
Like a picture, a rainbow-coloured blue sky
Flood over, earth, is dry.

Tom Mule
Holmer Green Senior School, Holmer Green

Russia Vs Ukraine

War
Something that goes on forever and ever
It never stops

It is made by disagreement
Hate, carelessness
If only it could end
But one day we may achieve world peace
No war
Or hate!

Russia vs Ukraine is the opposite of world peace
Hate, bombing, gun attacks
Why is it so hard to create peace?

It is like an argument but brutal
It is like an argument but causes death, protests and danger
Why can't people be kind, respectful or even leave each
other alone?
If people are offending you
Tell them to stop
But only if they carry on
Is when you start to attack
Even if they don't stop
You don't always need to react.

Ezaan Qureshi
Holmer Green Senior School, Holmer Green

Cost Of Living

The cost of petrol, electricity, rent, cars and water, all slowly going up bit by bit
People will end up not being able to pay for all this stuff
They might end up being homeless
So, whenever you turn your tap on, don't forget to turn it off
Otherwise, you'll waste loads of water
When you need petrol don't go buy petrol when you still have like 100 miles left
You could try not to buy a new car only buy it when you know 100% you need a new car
Or you could even buy an already used car
Don't buy takeaway all the time, try and make it yourself
You never know, you might even like making your own food.

Chester Styles
Holmer Green Senior School, Holmer Green

Hope

In the distance lies an island
Bleak and ominous
Shrouded in cloud and sombre gloom
This is where it hides
What they keep away is invisible to the untrained eye
Their troubles and worries are locked behind gates
While they search for someone to give the key
The key to their mind
The key to their soul

To see where it lies
Lonely, shrouded in its robe of abandonment
But the key glints
This is the glint of hope
A glint that can turn into a sparkle, to a shine
To a striking blaze as bright as the sun
And within the flame's warmth lies what they seek
Happiness and bliss
Bliss and happiness

Hope.

Oliver Sendall (12)
Holmer Green Senior School, Holmer Green

Bullying Is Wrong

A lways be kind as it will make someone's day,
N ever be a bully as one hurtful word can go a long way,
T hink about what you do before you do or say,
I n school should be a safe space,

B ullying is cruel, no one should bully, no one at all,
U nited I am and united I stay,
L et's live in peace,
L et there be light,
Y ou should stand up for yourself,
I f you bully you will get caught one day,
N ever fight back as it will get you in trouble too,
G o tell someone you trust.

Maisie Lomas (11)
Holmer Green Senior School, Holmer Green

Dear 7-Year-Old Me

Dear 7-year-old me
Shine bright like a star
Don't be ashamed to disagree
Never be afraid to be who you are

Dear the girl I used to be
Be kind to all around you
Show your true personality
No pressure to be the girl you once drew

Dear the child I see in the picture
Make others feel happiness
Don't mould yourself to fit the structure
Be thankful for those who carried us

Dear the kid I see within
Try your best to succeed
Don't let them get you down, lift your chin
You're a special person, indeed.

Lexie Vaughan (13)
Holmer Green Senior School, Holmer Green

Family

Family are there for you when you cry
Family are there for you when you like
Your sister gives you clothing advice
While your brothers just want to play games on your device

Your parents make you breakfast, lunch and dinner
When the time comes, they buy you Christmas and birthday presents
They pack your bag before school
They tuck you into bed at night

But then there are bad days
The days you argue with your siblings and get into fights
And later you apologise and everything is right
And in the end, you love your family, and your family loves you.

Nyiema Kidby (13)
Holmer Green Senior School, Holmer Green

Hopes And Dreams

H ow I wish they could see me now
O h how sad they would be
P lease forgive me they will say
E very day I remember what they said
S o how I wish I never believed

A nd here I am
N ever would I look back and say I should have done this, I should have done that
D on't doubt yourself

D on't listen to the haters
R each for the stars
E veryone should care
A nd should respect
M ost should appreciate
S omeone's hopes and dreams.

Mia James (12)
Holmer Green Senior School, Holmer Green

The Cost Of Living

I want the world to be a happy place to live

N ever have I ever thought about the cost of our lives

S adness is the past so let's shape the future

P ut a smile on the face of you or your friend

I nside we all know the mistakes we have made

R ight now is your opportunity to change and use your time

A t the moment we are trying but we need your help

T wo choices, be lazy or at least try and do something

I can do something! say to yourself

O r say it to a friend

N ever give up!

Felix Richardson (11)
Holmer Green Senior School, Holmer Green

Bullying

B ig people picking on you
U sing your fists won't get you through
L earn to ignore
L ie and you'll get more
Y ou should tell so they don't get to your core
I f you just ignore, you could get bullied more
N ever give up or you'll get more
G o and tell somebody so the bullies learn

I f it never stops
S hould you tell? Yes!

B ullies are jealous
A nd you're not
D o not let them win and the bullies will rot.

Ethan Odiam (12)
Holmer Green Senior School, Holmer Green

Incredible Island

Come follow me across my island
Stand here and watch the glorious view
Now sit here and sink away into the sunset
There's nowhere else I would rather be

Run, run, run, come follow me
Crashing waves that are sky blue
Blazing sun so near, yet out of reach
Feeling like I am skating on ice
So graceful and so elegant

Come to my house, the view is bliss
Where birds fly high, and dolphins jump
Where you can see waves come floating in
Where children play so happy, so young

Bye-bye my dear old friend, good to see you
Come and follow me soon around my sweet island.

Isla Worth
Holmer Green Senior School, Holmer Green

Hopes And Dreams

Hope can be found in the strangest of places,
the happy people in separate spaces,
Somewhere along the stony way,
A seed lay there from yesterday,

The seed pushes through the ground,
Not strong enough to bear a sound,
Hope is the feeling that carries you through,
And it is the future for the seed and you,

When I dream,
I think about a bright beam,
Passing through my windowpane,
It looks like a plane,

I want to be a pilot with a kind team
That's my dream.

Alicia Spinks-Gillen (12)
Holmer Green Senior School, Holmer Green

Peer Pressure

P eer pressure is never okay
E ven if you commit it alone
E xclude it from your own phone
R emember never, not even alone

P ush it out of real life
R emembering those who choose the fight
E veryone should stand against it
S hould you be the big bully or
S hould you be the hero
U sually you can put end to this
R ight now, this could end
E ven if you were a bully

You can change the world!

Harrison Garrett (11)

Holmer Green Senior School, Holmer Green

Fear

The noises you make
Causing me to feel unsafe
The excitement you cause
Makes me feel anxiety

You're hyper
You're excitable
You're loud
You're always off the ground

You're everything I dislike
You won't leave me be
You don't take notice
And keep doing this to me

You follow me around
You toss me to the ground
You will follow me everywhere
You aren't even aware

You jump
You bite
You give me a fright
You hold on to me tight

I hide and then you find
Everyone I go to
People want to know
What you are

A dog.

Katie Bickerton (12)
Holmer Green Senior School, Holmer Green

Earth's Magic

We live in a world of magic,
Full of danger, dragons and excitement,
Wizards working and weaving magic,
Wisdom in the clouds,
Magic and dragons touching the clouds,
And I don't want to lose that.

Dwarf caves roaring with echos,
Serpents slithering around the jungle,
However I've noticed that magic is disappearing,
I always check before bed,
The Earth's magic is the environment,
Save the magic,
Save the environment.

Ericka Fiske (12)
Holmer Green Senior School, Holmer Green

Environment

E ndangered animals
N uclear waste filling the sky
V iolence destroying nations and habitats
I llegal wildlife trade
R ivers becoming polluted
O il spills causing animal deaths
N o more plastic should enter our seas
M arine life is dying due to plastic in the ocean
E lectricity is becoming more popular
N ow causing coal to be burnt
T o create for us and to use for our pleasure.

George Smith (12)

Holmer Green Senior School, Holmer Green

Hard Work Beats Talent When Talent Doesn't Work Hard

H ard work beats talent when talent doesn't work hard
E veryone used to tell me
N ow I know it's true
D on't worry if you're not the best around
E ventually your dreams will come true
R e-watch Jordan Henderson
S o much hate he has overcome
O verall he is my idol above others
N ow as I said... hard work beats talent when talent doesn't work hard. He has proven it can be done.

Bobby Ardren (12)
Holmer Green Senior School, Holmer Green

Hopes And Dreams

We all have hopes and dreams
Which we start to achieve when we're teens
You have to use your imagination
All you need is determination

Hope is having a strong desire
Which could be as strong as fire
It's mainly about always believing
And having that feeling always increasing

Dreams are like having a goal
Which only you can control
It could be a fantasy
But it would always give you a feeling of supremacy.

Jayna Thohan (12)
Holmer Green Senior School, Holmer Green

Homophobia

Finger to finger,
hand to hand.
Sitting by the sea,
with their toes in the sand.

Everyone is equal,
no one is different.
We are all people,
gay lives matter.

We can't choose who others love,
the choice is up to them.
From Jeffree Star,
to Alan Turing from up above.

No need for homophobia,
it is irrelevant.
We are all equal,
this is important.

Gay Lives Matter
GLM.

Sophie Osborne (12)
Holmer Green Senior School, Holmer Green

Environment Poem

As the sun rises as does the flame,
It is not our fault, we claim.

The fire spreads like lies,
The leaves, the grass, the ground, cries.

As the fire blooms,
Dead trees loom.

After the night's lights show,
The forest is at an all-time low.

We know we have apologised, yet
The forest will never forget.

The fire's gone but the memory makes the grass
A little colder as you pass...

Hugo Scott-White (11)
Holmer Green Senior School, Holmer Green

Wouldn't It Be Bad...?

Wouldn't it be bad
if the sky was black and the icebergs were just melting?
Wouldn't it be bad
if the coasts were flooding and the earth started heating up?
Wouldn't it be bad
if habitats were gone and animals can't find some food?
Wouldn't it be bad
if food got destroyed and we can't eat them anymore?
Wouldn't it be bad
if this all happened?
So just take care of our environment!

Josh Fallon (12)
Holmer Green Senior School, Holmer Green

Nothing Left

Nobody has got the time to change the world each day.
No one seems to care where their plastic's thrown away.
Nobody thinks recycling once will make a difference
anyway.
No one knows that everything they do is such a waste.
They look at those poor animals and smoke in the sky...
They say they'll do things differently but later they won't try.
When the world comes to an end they'll think again and
they will cry.

Lucy Titchmarsh (11)
Holmer Green Senior School, Holmer Green

Missing Part Of Me

You live so far away
I met you in the long summer days
The memories you gave me in the last few days are now
here to stay
I ignored everyone's warnings
Because I could feel you calling
Calling me to stay
And not to fly away
I didn't say goodbye
And told you it was because I was shy
But in reality, I couldn't say
Because I knew we would meet again one day
I love you even though I can't stay.

Sophia Arshad (13)
Holmer Green Senior School, Holmer Green

Flooding

Water dripping down
The horizon started appearing
Drip. Drip. Drip
It's coming from the drains
The village crumbling down like dominoes
There was nothing to see except dust
The people who only have a bungalow
Would not like this
The water is one floor deep
People on top of their houses
Breaking gutters and spilling water across the street
Snap! Snap! Snap! Snap!
Then it finally happened...
Burst
The sound
It has got me
Argh!

Jack Mahoney (11)
Holmer Green Senior School, Holmer Green

Jealousy

Jealousy is that piquing of the soul
I'm not happy. Why not me? What is this test?
You let your brain take control
All the thoughts make you second guess

Suddenly you hate the way you feel
Hate the way you look
You try to fit the ideal
But as days pass by, time is stolen

Before, you were lonely as an abandoned house
You were scurrying for acceptance like a mouse
However, now you fit in just as yourself
Be who you are and not another self.

Iqra Iqbal (12)
Holmer Green Senior School, Holmer Green

Hallway Drama

Walking from classroom to classroom,
I wonder who I'll bump into today,
Maybe a close friend,
Maybe a teacher,
Or maybe one of the tall Year 10s
Who knows in these halls.
Being the smallest one here,
Squished between 10 other Year 10s,
I feel 3 feet tall,
In this big, chunky hall.
Where's M4,
No one can see,
Only the tall people can see,
In these big, chunky halls.

Jessica Macdonald (11)
Holmer Green Senior School, Holmer Green

The War

This was really bad.
Russia kept on going, bombs dropping and dropping and dropping overhead.
By now all of our soldiers were dead.
We had to keep on running and get to safety.
I was so hungry I could eat anything tasty.
We were nearly there, just one last push.
I could see everyone in the shelter, they were being helped by the helpers.
Finally we had made it and people welcomed us gracefully.

Annabelle Houghton (11)
Holmer Green Senior School, Holmer Green

Better Than A Tree

I think I will never see,
A poem better than a tree,
Destined for the chipping mill
Every leaf a dollar bill

That pale trunk, those slender limbs,
My imagination swims
I think I shall never see
Such a golden opportunity

It is the worst of sights
A living thing that has no rights
That is why I will never see
Anything more beautiful than a tree.

Ruben Myburgh (12)
Holmer Green Senior School, Holmer Green

Flooding

Water everywhere filling up the drains
Overflowing drains spilling out
Water slowly fills up the streets
People scared
People fled
People getting evacuated
Water rising higher and higher
Breaking gutters rushing down
It's so dangerous you could drown

Everyone is forced to leave
Everyone has the hope to come back
Everyone has awoken in different places
Looking at different faces
People's houses wrecked.

Skye Hopkins (11)

Holmer Green Senior School, Holmer Green

Be Yourself

No matter what people say, you can be what you want,
If someone is discouraging or doubting you don't let it
fool you,
Even if you do something wrong doesn't mean you can't
make it right,
If you are kind don't let anything or anyone take that away
from you,
You can be special in your own way,
No matter where you are or what you are doing,
Just be you.

Ayaan Qureshi (11)
Holmer Green Senior School, Holmer Green

Hopes And Dreams

Hopes and dreams,
Have you ever had a dream,
When it seems out of reach,
And impossible to achieve?

But you didn't give up,
You tried and tried again hoping for the best,
And you did it,
You did it,
You achieved what you thought was unachievable,
You have become the best you that you can be,
Proving those that doubted you wrong.

Niall Messer (12)
Holmer Green Senior School, Holmer Green

In Search Of Peace

Away from the racket of busy urban life
Away from the polluted cloudy skies
I want to breathe in the fresh scent of autumn, in the breeze
I want to hear the honeyed trill of distant birds
I want to immerse myself in the silence of my surroundings
I want to absorb the beauty of the valley's scenery
I want to touch the dewy leaves
I want my soul to flow with the sparkling stream.

Zaina Ahmed (13)
Holmer Green Senior School, Holmer Green

On My Island

On my island
The sea is clear
The skies are a beautiful blue
And there are foxes and deer

On my island
The trees dance
The sun leaps from the clouds
And all the animals prance

On my island
The clouds are as white as snow
And as fluffy as marshmallows
You won't ever want to go!

On my island
The trees grow tall
The divine dolphins dive into the waves
My island is for all!

Anna Lacey (12)
Holmer Green Senior School, Holmer Green

Go And Achieve Your Dreams

B ullying is bad

U psets people too and is not cool or funny

L isten to people around you

L et's make a change

Y ou are nasty, why can't you just play on swings or play with strings?

I t's not cool to be cruel

N ever look back, no one deserves to be bullied

G et the best out of life.

Dylan Whitticase (11)

Holmer Green Senior School, Holmer Green

Autumn Is Coming

Trees crashing down
Crash! Crash! Crash!
Leaves falling on each other on the floor
Water falling on them and splashing up at my legs
You could tell that autumn was coming
I could smell the damp air all around me
I peered around, looking for someone but no one was there
Bright lights beamed through the clouds as the sun shone
on me.

Archie Groves (11)
Holmer Green Senior School, Holmer Green

My Darkened Heart

When will I feel accepted?
When will I know the smiles are genuine?
"It's all harmless," they say
"It's just words," they say
But we both know better

Their words follow me around
Poised to sink into my skin
Infecting my heart
Seeping the joy out of me
They follow me around
Never seeming to let go
Plunging me into a world of my own darkness.

Yasmin Arshad (12)
Holmer Green Senior School, Holmer Green

Arsenal

We're at the top of the table, were having a ball
We just can't fall
We walk up and down the stands, watch them with faith
We just have to wait
Welcome to Arsenal where miracles happen
We just have to trust our captain
As they run up and down the lines
We watch them shine
We believe in you
Come on Arsenal.

Oliver Edwards (11)
Holmer Green Senior School, Holmer Green

Amazing Words

A lways try your hardest
M ake sure you push yourself
A lways try to give something rather than giving nothing
Z en feelings are incredible, try to make yourself feel like that
I nstead of saying I can't do it, say I can't do it 'yet'
N ever give up
G ive the best work you can.

Alishba Mudassar (11)
Holmer Green Senior School, Holmer Green

The Environment

E verything gone, trees falling
N o one to help
V ery sad animals screaming hello
I f anyone would help
R hinos would be proud
O n and on the day goes
N o one comes
M y place called home
E very day
N early gone
T he trees are all gone.

Megan Howse (12)
Holmer Green Senior School, Holmer Green

The Future

Nobody even thinks about the future because it's too far away
But it's right around the corner.
Some adults don't care about our future
And think they don't have to do anything but we depend on them
And their actions will depend on our future
And their acts will depend on climate change
Adults... it's up to you.

Jude Stenning (11)
Holmer Green Senior School, Holmer Green

Bullying Needs To End

B ullying needs to end
U nnecessary cruelty isn't kind
L iving with people like this is not easy
L et's make this place a better place
Y ou are the person to fix this place
I gnoring bullying you should not do
N o more bullying
G o help the world.

Archie Fairchild (12)

Holmer Green Senior School, Holmer Green

Social Media

Social media controls you
It changes you, it torments you
People make rude comments
Which leads to people being insecure
And also leads people to do bad things to themselves
This could be stopped by being kinder
And caring about other people's feelings, not just your own
Think before you speak!

Aaivee-Elizabeth Kelly (11)
Holmer Green Senior School, Holmer Green

The Future

T he future is neat
H ere it is a beat
E veryone never retreats

F or everyone isn't a priest
U sernames are unleashed
T he people ate sweets
U ltra heroes do the beats
R ooms are now beefed
E verywhere is ungreased.

William Fiske (13)
Holmer Green Senior School, Holmer Green

Young Love

We are done
Over
I feel lifeless
There's no cure

I gave everything
I tried
Things I didn't know I could give
Doors I didn't know could be opened

In another, we will be destined
All the tears have dried up
Now there's nothing but hope.

Grace Porter (13)
Holmer Green Senior School, Holmer Green

Hope, Peace, Love And Light

Hope, peace, love and light,
Everything for tonight,
Love each other and your friends,

All I want is peace and love,
Don't you want that too?
I do hope you want it too,

All is done with light and hope,
So enough with war,
We don't want it any more.

Izzy Beaumont (11)
Holmer Green Senior School, Holmer Green

Don't Be Racist

R acism is shocking
A ll of it needs to stop
C an you imagine being treated poorly because of the colour of your skin?
I f you are racist you need to stop!
S ome people go to jail
M aybe think twice before you speak.

Joe Latham (12)
Holmer Green Senior School, Holmer Green

Racism

R ight now people are suffering
A round most places in the world
C aused by racism
I t is heartbreaking, a vile act
S o don't be racist
M any people in the world are hurting because of discrimination.

Idris Syed (12)
Holmer Green Senior School, Holmer Green

Winter Is Here

Snowflakes fall softly
Crunch! goes the ground underfoot
Breathe in the fresh air

The trees are bare and sleeping
The woods are very peaceful

Icicles gleaming
Dreaming of hot chocolate
The winter is here.

Lydia Beaumont (13)
Holmer Green Senior School, Holmer Green

Future

F uel or electric
U nderpopulation or overpopulation
T o understand me
U nderstand each other or war will start
R ainforests or no forests
E xpensive things destroy lives
S top war now!

Luis Tebbett (11)
Holmer Green Senior School, Holmer Green

Weather

Splash! Bang!
Bright flashes in the sky
Fires in the trees
Starving families
Forced to leave our flooded homes
Schools closed
For good?
Acid falling from the sky
Climate change
Hurricanes destroying precious homes
Is it the end?

Megan Newell (11)
Holmer Green Senior School, Holmer Green

Global Warming

Global warming is a bummer
Get ready for a hot summer
It is very surprising
How fast the heat is rising
The ice caps are melting
What can you do to be helping?
Polar bears are dying
People are crying.

Darcy Flight (12)
Holmer Green Senior School, Holmer Green

Beach

The sun beaming down, shining off the ocean
And the waves crash landing on the sand
The yellow sand swallows me as I lay and watch
The sunlight. People laugh and run in the ocean
While the waves are trying to push them back.

Daanyal Shafaqat (11)
Holmer Green Senior School, Holmer Green

Racism

R acism is real
A wful to feel
C ops are out to kill
I 'm here to stop them kill
S o people help me
M any of you have helped as we will succeed.

Ryan Roberts (12)
Holmer Green Senior School, Holmer Green

World War

Planes flying in acolyte sky
Bang! Bang! Bang!
Pattering gunshots on the German planes
Bombs dropping on the cities
Planes crashing
Germans harming animals and people
Tanks firing bullets.

Callum Lewis (12)
Holmer Green Senior School, Holmer Green

Werewolf

All the people were scared
Of the werewolves
The beasts were hairy
Had sharp teeth and hairy fur
There were different types of them
They had a king called King Bloodeye.

Djimon Sifflet

Holmer Green Senior School, Holmer Green

Forest Fires

Forest fires are no good
It is burning the wood
The foxes flee to the bush
It is not good
Don't just stand there
The poor bears are in despair
It's not good
Help save the wood.

Thomas Hatch (11)
Holmer Green Senior School, Holmer Green

Environment

The forest so green,
Destroyed because of our greed,
One leaf wasted because of a sheet,
One piece of paper made from that tree,
That will destroy a home for a bee.

Aaron Christie
Holmer Green Senior School, Holmer Green